BUILDING MATERIALS FOR LIFE

BUILDING MATERIALS
for Life

Radical Common Sense, The Power of Right Thinking,
Relevant Religion, Plowing New Ground, Persistence, and
35 other essays on how to enhance your life

MILLARD FULLER

Founder and President of Habitat for Humanity International

SMYTH&HELWYS
PUBLISHING, INCORPORATED   MACON, GEORGIA

Smyth & Helwys Publishing, Inc.
6316 Peake Road
Macon, Georgia 31210-3960
1-800-747-3016
©2002 by Smyth & Helwys Publishing
All rights reserved.
Printed in the United States of America.

Photo Credits: John Curry, Kim MacDonald

The paper used in this publication meets the
minimum requirements of American National
Standard for Information Sciences—Permanence
of Paper for Printed Library Materials.
ANSI Z39.48–1984. (alk. paper)

Cataloging-in-Publication Data
on file with the Library of Congress

ACKNOWLEDGMENTS

This book has been a team effort.

I started writing it in October 2001. Most of the writing was completed by February 2002. Then I shared the manuscript with my special assistant, Joy Holloway, and with other fellow Habitat people, Jill Claflin, Kathryn Reid, Kimberly Moore, and with my wife Linda and daughter, Faith. All of them made corrections and offered valuable advice on how to improve the manuscript.

Next, I gave the manuscript to Carla Robinson, a dedicated and talented young woman in our communications department. She dug into this project and made an incredible difference in the final product. She renamed chapters, reorganized them, divided the book into five distinct sections, deleted some things and added others. In short, she was wonderful. Indeed, she was like an angel and words are inadequate with which to thank her.

Another awesome person on the team was my assistant Sharon Tarver. She typed and retyped the manuscript countless times, always without complaint and with great care and skill. I have a great love and appreciation for Sharon!

Finally, I want to thank Smyth & Helwys, publisher of the book. Especially, I want to express gratitude to Cecil and Catherine Staton, David Cassady, Keith Gammons, and the editorial staff, all of whom worked with diligence and skill to produce a quality publication and to get it out in record time.

Millard Fuller

To Linda, my precious wife and life partner, and to our children, Chris, Kim, Faith, and Georgia, our beloved daughter-in-law, Dianne, and cherished sons-in-law, Jim Isakson and Manfred Ludi, and our grandchildren, Benjamin, Joshua, Zachary, Alexander, Sophie, and Jasmine.

FOREWORD

For much of my life, I have been involved in building things. When I was a boy, my father had a farm near our home in the small cotton-mill town of Lanett, Alabama. We were often at that farm building a barn or repairing a tenant house or putting up a fence.

While a student at Auburn University, I worked part of one summer building houses in Michigan. Also, at that time my dad had some rental houses in our hometown, and I was frequently engaged on weekends putting on a roof, building a porch, or some other such projects in connection with those houses.

In law school at the University of Alabama, I started a business venture with a fellow student. As we generated profits, we invested in rental houses. My partner and I did a lot of "hands-on" repairs and renovations of those units.

Then, after a few years of practicing law and running a business in Montgomery, Alabama, my wife, Linda, and I embarked on a new path in life, which eventually led us to a small Christian community near Americus, Georgia. There, we helped start a housing program called

"Partnership Housing." That was the beginning of what has become Habitat for Humanity.

So, for the past three plus decades of my life, I have been concerned about building on almost a daily basis.

In all of the building I have done over the years—whether putting up a barn, adding a porch to a tenant house, digging holes for fence posts and stretching barbed wire, or building a Habitat house—I have learned that the first thing one must do is find and get together the necessary building materials and tools. To build a fence, for example, you need fence posts, barbed wire, staples, post hole diggers, a hammer, barbed wire stretchers, wire cutters, and a dirt compactor to tamp in the dirt around the fence posts. More materials and tools are needed to build a house. And nothing is more frustrating than to get started on a building project and learn that some essential building material is missing.

Just as materials are needed for a building project, in like manner, materials are necessary for building a human life.

Did you know that you are "God's building"? In 1 Corinthians 3:9-10, the Apostle Paul writes, "We are laborers together with God; you are God's field, God's building. According to the grace of God given to me, like a skilled master builder I laid a foundation, and someone else is building on it. Each builder must choose with care how to build on it."

Are you building with care as you build your life? Do you have the right materials for building? What do you have and what's missing?

This little collection of forty essays is an attempt to stimulate thinking about building materials like the following that you need for enhancing and building your life:

Attitude. Starting with a right attitude is absolutely essential to building a good fence, a strong barn, a beautiful house, or a meaningful life.

Perseverance. Are you a quitter or do you stay the course? Perseverance is a crucial building material for repairing a derelict house or for bolstering a life that has run into challenges.

Fear and Doubt. Every person is plagued with these two emotions at various times throughout life. How do you deal with them? Do they immobilize you or do you work through those problem situations? Do you get bogged down in life? How do you extricate yourself from whatever is holding you back?

The above and many more topics are covered in this book. Together, they comprise "building materials" for a better life. I hope you enjoy going through this material. I fervently hope and pray that you find what you need to improve and strengthen your life. Most of all, as you search and as you build, I hope you are brought closer to the Master Builder who will guide you in building the very best life possible.

Millard Fuller
Americus, Georgia
Summer 2002

TABLE OF CONTENTS

FUNDAMENTALS

FAITH

CHALLENGES

LIFE LESSONS

GIFTS

FUNDAMENTALS

One ship drives east and another west
With the selfsame winds that blow.
'Tis the set of the sails and not the gales
Which tell us the way to go.
Like the winds of the sea are the ways of fate,
As we voyage along through life;
'Tis the set of the soul that decides its goal
And not the calm or the strife.

— *Ella Wheeler Wilcox*

ATTITUDE

When I was a boy growing up in the east Alabama cotton-mill town of Lanett, I had a schoolteacher named Lucy Meadows. All of the students called her "Miss Lucy." She had silver-white hair and was quite stern. If a student misbehaved beyond a certain point, she would have that student hold out his or her hand. Miss Lucy would take hold of the fingers of the extended hand with her left hand and then, with her right hand, whack the open palm three or four times with a twelve-inch ruler. The resulting burning sensation lasted for several minutes and definitely had an effect on future behavior!

Miss Lucy also talked a lot about the importance of attitude in life, usually right after whacking someone with the ruler. She would hold forth on other subjects as well, but attitude was her favorite topic. "Attitude," she would say again and again, "is everything."

At that time I didn't get it. I thought to myself, "That old woman doesn't know what she's talking about. Attitude means nothing. What's important is whether or not you know the answers on the next test."

Over the years, though, I've come to realize the great wisdom of what Miss Lucy taught us. Attitude is everything. From attitude flows action.

Attitude colors how we relate to people around us and how we think about ourselves. If you have a negative attitude about yourself, and believe that you are not capable of doing something, you will probably fail. Conversely, if you believe in yourself and think positively about your ability and intelligence, you will find yourself amazingly capable. Likewise, if you have a positive attitude about those around you, your relationships will be more successful and people will tend to respond more positively to you. If you have an attitude that problems confronted in life probably have a solution, you will most likely find or create one.

But what if you find that you have a bad attitude? How do you change for the positive? I believe the answer lies in thinking about it. You've obviously got to want to change before any change will occur. And one also must realize that old attitudes and habits that are deeply ingrained, perhaps over many years, do not give way to new and better attitudes by magic.

Celebrated author and lecturer Charles Swindoll has written often and powerfully about attitude. "The longer I live the more convinced I become that life is 10 percent what happens to us and 90 percent how we respond to it."[1] He concludes that we cannot change our past or the inevitable or the fact that people will act in a certain way. The only thing we can do is to be in charge of our attitudes.

Perhaps you could write down three things about your attitude that you would like to improve. What changes can you make in life to change your attitude for the better? If you have a negative attitude, what is causing it? Your job? A conflict with friends or a family member? What do you need to do to deal with those causes and conflicts in your life? Hard work, determination, and a desire to change will bring about a transformation in attitude. Prayer and meditation on forming a positive outlook will ensure the result you desire.

Miss Lucy, you got it right. Attitude is everything. Thanks for your great gift.

Improve your attitude to improve your life.

Note

[1] Charles Swindoll, *Attitude: Your Most Important Choice* (Anaheim CA: Insight for Living, 2000), 5.

THE POWER OF RIGHT THINKING

One day when I was a student at the University of Alabama Law School, I dozed off in a criminal law class. The professor, Sam Beatty, noticed that I was asleep, so he asked me a question. Of course, I had no idea what the answer was because I hadn't been listening to the lecture. I didn't even hear the question.

Professor Beatty savored the moment. "Look, class! There's old Fuller over there thinking, always thinking!" I was totally embarrassed and immediately wide awake.

Thinking is so important. And yet, so many people spend so little time thinking. We are asleep or our attention is diverted by other things. We are surrounded by distractions: blaring radios, televisions, traffic, sirens. The list goes on.

The book of Proverbs in the Bible says that "as a person thinks in his heart, so is he" (23:7). So, what if a person goes through life basically thinking about nothing of significance? What is he or she? The answer is obvious.

How many times have you asked a friend or colleague what they are thinking about and the dull answer comes back, "Nothing"? Wrong thoughts can be even worse than a blank mind. I was in church one Sunday when I was dating my soon-to-be wife, Linda. I whispered to her, "Do you know what I'm thinking about?"

"What?" she whispered back.

"A million dollars."

I should have been listening to the pastor and concentrating my thoughts on God, but I was devoting my mental attention to money. It was a classic example of how money crowds God out of one's mind.

Jesus said that a person cannot serve God and money. He will hate the one and love the other, or else he will be loyal to the one and despise the other. To serve something or someone requires thought devoted to that entity. Again, Jesus said it is difficult for a rich person to enter into the Kingdom. Why would he say something like that? I believe it is because the more possessions one accumulates, the more thinking time is devoted to them. If a person has multiple cars, boats, acres of land, houses, all kinds of investments and other possessions, it takes a lot of time to make sure everything is secure and well taken care of. No time is left for God. People who are not so encumbered with numerous possessions have thinking time available for spiritual matters.

I remember reading about the great missionary and literacy leader, Frank Laubach. He was working among Muslim people in the far south of the Philippines. He was living in a mountainous area and he had very few physical possessions. Laubach had abundant time to reflect and to think about God. He decided one day that he would try to think about God *all the time*. He knew he would have to devote mental energy to things like cooking, eating, bathing, and going about his other daily activities, but he determined never to allow God to be out of his thoughts. At first, he said, it was really hard to think about God all the time. He would go along, thinking hard about God and, after a while, he would realize that God was totally out of his thoughts. He would struggle to bring God back to the center of his thinking. He related that as he continued the struggle, it became easier, over time, to stay focused on God.

My wife, Linda, and I have four children and six grandchildren. Our oldest child is our son, Chris. He and his wife, Dianne, have two boys, Benjamin and Joshua. One day Chris was in their car with Benjamin, headed to the mall. They were chatting away. After a while Benjamin fell silent, but Chris continued to talk. Finally, Ben turned to his father and exclaimed, "Be quiet, Dad! I'm thinking about God."

I believe it is important to spend quality, quiet time just to think, not only about God, but about other subjects as well. The mind should be cleared as much as possible to make room for serious thinking.

Pick a subject. Your marriage. Is it fulfilling? How is the relationship? Do you communicate well? What needs improvement?

Your children. How are they doing? Do you spend enough time with them? What are you doing to enhance and improve your relationship with your children?

Your career. Are you successful or struggling? Is it in line with who you are? Are you headed in the right direction and pursuing your life's work?

Your city. Your country. The world situation. Your charitable giving. Your church. The company you work for and so forth.

If you will spend quality time thinking about various things that concern you, you'll be amazed at the insights you'll have. Indeed, thinking enriches one's life.

Finally, did you know that God thinks about you? The Bible says that the most humble person is of concern to God. Psalm 40:17, reads, "I am poor and needy; yet the Lord thinks upon me. You are my help and my deliverer; do not delay, O my God."

The Lord "thinks upon you." Isn't that a comforting thought? If God thinks about you, then you certainly should spend some serious time thinking about Him and about other matters that are of concern in your life.

Serious, directed, and concentrated right thinking is time well spent. It also inevitably results in helping to solve problems in your life. The French philosopher Voltaire once said that no problem can withstand an assault of sustained thinking. Choose one thing right now to think about that can enhance your life and the lives of those closest to you. Then, choose one other thing to think about that can enhance the lives of others very distant or very different from yourself. Finally, think about some aspect of your relationship with God.

Right thinking leads to right relationships and right actions.

LISTEN TO WHAT YOU SAY

Did you ever stop to think that you hear everything you say? Every thoughtful word, every dirty joke, every hateful utterance, every tender word of love that has ever come out of your mouth has been heard by your ears and registered in your brain. You are the only person in the world who can say that. Other people have heard many of the things you have said. A spouse or close friend has heard, perhaps, thousands upon thousands of your words. But you have heard everything.

I do a lot of public speaking, especially about Habitat for Humanity. I am committed to that work and feel privileged to be a part of the exciting venture of hammering out faith and love. Even so, sometimes I get bored hearing myself say the same thing over and over. To deal with that problem, I usually speak without notes. As a result, I often surprise and even delight myself with what I say. A stream of consciousness flows from my mouth and my ears hear every word. I even find myself getting inspired all over again from my own enthusiastic speeches.

One of the most dramatic stories I've ever heard concerning a person influencing himself with his own words is that of Irving Harris. Irving was a very dedicated Christian leader who lived much of his life in Princeton,

New Jersey. For several years he was editor of *Faith at Work* magazine. I got to know Irving when I lived and worked in New York several years ago. We remained close friends until his death some years later.

One day Irving was reminiscing about his youthful years, and he told me how he became a Christian. He was attending a church youth camp. The camp counselor came to Irving one morning and said that he wanted him to be the devotional speaker at vespers that evening. Irving said he was so terrified by the idea that he was speechless. Before he could respond, the counselor had turned on his heels and was gone.

Irving retreated to his cabin and suffered throughout the day, reading the Bible and struggling with what he would say that evening. He had never decided what he believed about Christ and had never made any kind of profession of faith.

When evening came, Irving stood to speak. He said the evening was absolutely perfect. The temperature was ideal. There was a slight breeze that made a soft, wonderful sound blowing through the pine trees. And the breeze made shimmering ripples on the surface of the lake that was immediately adjacent to the site of the vespers.

Irving said he waxed eloquent. His stirring and passionate words went not only to the ears of the other young people, they went to his own ears and to his heart. Right then and there, he decided to be a Christian. He determined to follow Christ as best he could. His own words converted him!

So, what you say is incredibly important because you influence yourself more than anyone else in the world. Think good thoughts and speak uplifting, positive words.

When I was in business and a law practice in Montgomery, Alabama, soon after graduating from the University of Alabama Law School, I realized that my business and law partner and I had gotten into the habit of using a lot of profanity. Over time, we literally saturated our speech with curse words. We could hardly say "Good morning" without an oath. After a while, the cursing became oppressive. A heaviness hung in the air. My partner and I decided that this practice had to cease. We held each other accountable and, within a few weeks, we were talking without the onerous curse words. I've never fallen into that habit again.

What is in your speech that should cease? What is missing from your conversations that should be added? Remember that you hear everything you say and you are influenced by it. Of course, you influence those around you with your words as well. So, make sure you influence yourself and others in a good and positive way with good and positive words.

Right now, say something positive and see how it feels!

PRAY FOR WISDOM

Give your servant an understanding heart—that I may discern between good and evil. (1 Kings 3:9)

The above prayer was uttered by King Solomon. It is his famous prayer asking for wisdom, which God answered. The Lord said to Solomon,

> Because you have asked this thing, and have not asked long life for yourself, nor have asked riches for yourself, nor have asked the life of your enemies, but have asked for yourself understanding to discern justice, behold I have done according to your words; see, I have given you a wise and understanding heart, so that there has not been anyone like you before you, nor shall any like you arise after you. (1 Kings 3:11-12)

Soon thereafter, two women came to Solomon, each claiming a little child as her own. Solomon heard the case and then asked for a sword as he prepared to cut the child in two with each woman getting half. One woman wailed, exclaiming that the child should go to the other woman. The other alleged mother coldly asked the king to cut the child apart as he had proposed. She wanted her half and the other woman could have the other half. Solomon saw immediately that the grieving woman was the true mother because she would rather have seen the other woman have the child than see it killed. So, Solomon gave the child to the rightful mother.

That's wisdom. And it comes from God.

One can get knowledge at a college or university. All kinds of information can be found on the Internet. But wisdom only comes from God. And it is highly desirable to have a wise and understanding heart, especially when important decisions must be made.

I recall hearing a story about a new college president who confronted a serious problem at his school soon after he was sworn in. It seems that speeding on campus was an urgent matter that needed attention. At a staff meeting, he ordered that speed bumps be installed throughout the campus. He was sure that would solve the problem.

An older member of the staff pointed out that a holiday was coming up very shortly and the students would leave campus. The staff member suggested that the speed bumps could be installed during the holiday and, when the students returned, the matter would be a *fait accompli*. The staff member wisely pointed out that if the speed bumps were put down while the students were on campus, there might be a negative reaction.

The new president bristled at the suggestion that some students might respond negatively to the installation of the speed bumps. "Put them down," he ordered. "I'm the president and I want to stop this foolishness now!" So the speed bumps were installed within a few days. That very night, a group of students ripped them up.

The older and wiser staff member was right: just having the power to do something doesn't mean that it is wise to exercise that power. Having patience and being a bit wiser would have gotten a better result. But I'm sure the new president learned a lesson.

As president and CEO of Habitat for Humanity International, I always counsel that wisdom should be sought persistently and diligently. And, since wisdom comes from God, prayer should be a regular part of all activities and decisions to be made in the ministry.

A great variety of situations arise in the multifaceted work of Habitat for Humanity. It is not always clear what the best courses of action are. I well remember a difficult matter that arose in one of our affiliates in south

Florida. A piece of land was secured on which a number of Habitat houses were to be built. The neighbors learned about the plan and made loud objections as they went to city council meetings and strongly opposed the Habitat plans.

"Those people," they argued, "will ruin our community. They are poor. They will throw trash everywhere. They are probably thieves, drug users, and other criminal types. We don't want them in our area."

The wise executive director of the Habitat affiliate, Lew Frazar, decided to take bold action. The affiliate had already chosen the families to live in the houses. He simply went with a few of those people from house to house, knocking on doors and introducing the new families to the people in the neighborhood. In effect, Lew said, "These are the people you don't like. Meet them and see for yourself that they are good people. Just like you and your family, they desire a good place to live."

The people of the neighborhood were convinced. I was in that community for a workweek some time thereafter and Lew pointed out to me several of the objecting neighbors who were on the site helping build the houses. A wise approach brought about the desired result.

Sometimes, prayer for a wise solution to a problem ends up with a dramatic and unexpected result. A few years ago, a serious matter arose in Quimbaya, Colombia, when the mayor advised the local Habitat leaders that she wanted to choose the families for future Habitat houses. The Habitat leaders patiently explained to the mayor that a crucial aspect of Habitat's mission is that the selection of families must be nondiscriminatory and without political or religious favor. Therefore, the selection of families must be made by an impartial group of local citizens, not by a political person who would likely show political favoritism.

The mayor was adamant. "I must choose the families or you are forbidden to build any more houses." The very successful program that was building a large number of houses came to a screeching halt. The local Habitat leaders contacted the national Habitat office in Bogotá and explained the crisis. Some of those leaders came to Quimbaya, and the two groups of Habitat officials had a long and serious prayer meeting asking for God's guidance. The following morning, the officials awoke to find the mayor had passed away during the night. In an interesting coincidence, the new mayor was named "Jesus."

Linda and I were in Quimbaya soon after the new mayor took office. He was totally cooperative with the local Habitat people, and building had returned to a full-scale operation.

The book of James in the New Testament offers this sound advice: "If any of you lacks wisdom, let him ask of God, who gives to all liberally and without reproach, and it will be given to him" (1:5).

So, ask for wisdom in seeking to know how to deal with difficult situations. God is listening and will bless you with an understanding heart.

Act on your good intentions and God will be with you.

EXTEND YOUR SPIRITUAL ANTENNAE

Clarence Jordan, founder of Koinonia Farm near Americus, Georgia, and my spiritual mentor, constantly astounded me with his keen insights. He seemed always to have a different perspective from other people on most subjects.

How he thought about God, for example, was not the classic "up in Heaven" concept. He envisioned God in a personal, intimate way and he got this way of thinking from Jesus. Clarence pointed out that when Jesus prayed, he spoke to God as "Daddy." The relationship was close and personal—God was real and "right here."

Clarence thought of God not only as a Heavenly Father but as a *partner*. He said that the wise seeker after God should extend his spiritual antennae to pick up God's messages. "God is broadcasting," Clarence would say, "and if we are listening, we can hear what He is saying."

Clarence said that God is the *senior partner* in the spiritual relationship and we are the *junior associates*. God actively seeks partners on earth to work with Him to carry out His heavenly plans.

Too often, Clarence continued, people make their own plans and then ask God to bless them. That's backwards, Clarence would intone. God doesn't bless *our* plans. He wants us to be His partners in carrying out His agenda.

In the United States, people often sing "God Bless America." This song is loved and passionately sung both at religious and secular events, and is especially popular during periods of national crisis. Of course, any right-thinking person would want God to bless us. But, I fear that the implication is, and the desire is, for God to *bless us, above others* or to the exclusion of others. That thinking is precisely backward, according to the thinking of Clarence Jordan. To get it right and to be in line with putting God first and not our own agenda or interests, maybe we need a new song, "America, Bless God." That is to say, America, and the people of America, extend your spiritual antennae to pick up God's messages. Then, live and act in accordance with those messages so that God will be pleased and blessed.

When Linda and I and our children moved to Koinonia in 1968 to launch a new ministry with Clarence and others at the farm, it was after a serious time of prayer and meditation. Clarence and I sensed strongly that God was calling us to work together to launch a new ministry. In obedience to that call, we moved our family to south Georgia. Soon thereafter, Clarence and I called together a group of dedicated friends to think and pray with us to better discern God's will for the proposed new venture. After three days of intensive sessions, we sensed clarity about the direction of the new thrust of Koinonia. It would be preaching, teaching, and application.

Clarence, especially, would preach across the land, urging people to listen to God and become His partners. Discipleship schools would be organized to go into more depth about God's will and way of doing things on earth. Finally, at Koinonia, we would try to put these partnership ideas into practice with three programs—Partnership Farming, Partnership Industries, and Partnership Housing.

In the following months, all of the above were implemented. Clarence crisscrossed the country, preaching to large and small crowds of people, mostly in church settings. Discipleship schools were planned and held in New York and other places, including Koinonia.

Farming of peanuts, soybeans, corn, and other crops was activated with white and black partners working together. Several small "industries" were set up, including a sewing plant to make women's pants and an oper-ation to produce tie-dyed apparel. A housing partnership plan was launched, whereby houses were to be built with and for nearby families who were living in shacks. Modest houses would be built and sold to those needy families at no profit with no interest, in keeping with the biblical teaching not to charge interest to the poor (see Exodus 22:25).

On October 29, 1969, just as all of the above programs were getting into full swing, Clarence was sitting at his desk in his "writing shack" out in a nearby field, preparing a sermon to be delivered at Mercer University in Macon, Georgia, when God called him home. He just leaned his head against the wall and breathed his last breath. He had had a massive heart attack at age 57.

As director of Koinonia, I had the wonderful privilege of conducting his burial service. I read from his "Cotton Patch" translation of the Scripture, using sections that emphasized partnership with God. The vers-es I selected were from what Clarence called 1 Jack and 1 Rock (1 John and 1 Peter). A portion of what I read follows:

> In order that you all, too, might be our partners, we are plainly telling you about something that's real, something that we have ourselves heard, that we have seen with our own two eyes. It's about the idea of life that we looked at and even felt with our own hands. Now the life took shape and we saw it and we are giving you our word and plainly telling you about the spiritual life which was with the Father and which took place in front of us. Our partnership then, is with the Father and with His Son, Jesus Christ. We are recording this so that the joy of us all may be completely full.[1]

In the months and years following Clarence's death, Koinonia's min-istry has continued, changing in various ways over the years. The part-nership enterprises in farming and industries eventually were closed, but the partnership housing program evolved into Habitat for Humanity.

After nearly five years at Koinonia, Linda and I took the idea of part-nership housing to Africa, where we built houses for three years in Zaire (now the Democratic Republic of the Congo). Then, we returned to Americus and set up Habitat for Humanity in 1976 as a separate nonprofit organization to build houses around the world, patterned on the

Partnership Housing program at Koinonia. In 1977 international head-quarters were established in the town of Americus and the work has steadily expanded around the world. By 2002 more than 130,000 houses had been built for more than 650,000 people.

Along the way, partnership with God and with a host of diverse other partners has been emphasized. Every morning at Habitat headquarters, the day starts with a time of devotions and prayer. We have always want-ed to seek God's guidance in all that we do. That partnership is para-mount, and God has been faithful. Over the years those of us involved in the work have diligently sought to be faithful, with our spiritual antennae always extended to receive God's messages.

Are your spiritual antennae extended so that you can receive God's messages that are broadcast for you? Or are you simply going through life with no regard for God's ideas and messages?

I am convinced that the far wiser approach to life is to be *sensitive* and *receptive* to whatever messages or instruction God may have for you. I would urge you to put up your spiritual antennae. I believe you will be amazed and blessed by the guidance you receive.

Note

[1] Clarence Jordan, *The Cotton Patch Version of Hebrews and the General Epistles* (Clinton NJ: New Win Publishing Inc., 1969), 75.

DON'T FIGHT PROBLEMS—SOLVE THEM!

When I was a student at Auburn University, I attended a lecture that was part of a "Religious Emphasis" week. The speaker was talking about problem solving. He said, "When you've got a problem, don't fight the problem—solve it!" That simple insight, that profound bit of wisdom has helped me enormously all throughout my life.

Quite often, when confronted with a problem, the great temptation is to "go into battle" against the problem. When that happens, the problem often wins. Nothing changes for the better; frustration and anger rule the day. The problem emerges victorious.

A young woman came to my office one day to talk about a serious problem she had encountered at her previous place of employment. She explained that she was working in a home for people with mental impairments. It was work that she loved, and she had developed a deep bond with the people under her care. She had observed, though, that their daily life was largely devoid of any sense of excitement. She decided to have a festive party for her mentally impaired friends. She gathered them around her and explained what she had in mind. They were ecstatic, she told me.

Planning got under way immediately. She had never seen such joy and enthusiasm.

Planning continued and excitement grew. Finally, the big event was just a few days away. Abruptly, her supervisor came in and announced that she couldn't have the party because he felt that it would not be good for the people in the home to get so stimulated. The young woman was devastated. She had poured so much energy into the planned party, and she was positive that it would be so good and so encouraging to the people in her care. She tried to get her supervisor to change his mind, but he was adamant. No party.

She paused in the telling of her story. "So," I asked, "What did you do?"

"I resigned. I just couldn't stand what that guy did. I quit and left immediately."

"Did your resignation cause the supervisor to allow the party?"

"Well, no, it didn't," she admitted.

"Then what did your resignation accomplish?"

"What do you mean?"

"I mean, did your resignation accomplish anything other than getting you out of the picture? Did your leaving make things better for the people you cared for so much? Were they helped in any way?"

"Well, no."

"Let me tell you what you did. You were confronted with a problem and you fought it. Your way of 'fighting' was to leave. You didn't solve a thing. Next time think more about a solution rather than fighting the problem."

Problems usually have solutions. That is true and that is what one should keep in mind when confronted with a problem. When Linda and I were living and working in Africa as missionaries, we were constantly confronted with problems of various kinds. One such problem arose immediately upon our arrival. We got there all right, but our barrels of household goods did not. Linda didn't have a pan for baking biscuits. So, she found a dustpan, which she cleaned up, and—presto—she could make biscuits for the family.

In the course of working in the house-building program, which I launched in Mbandaka, Zaire (now the Democratic Republic of the

Congo), the truck that was used to transport blocks from the block-making plant to the construction site broke down. Parts needed for repair work were not readily available, so it seemed that we were stuck.

I searched for an alternate way to transport the blocks and found a tractor with a wagon. That method of transport was used until the tractor broke down. Once again, it seemed that we were stuck. But, I simply hired a group of men with push carts, and we did not lose a bit of our building momentum as the needed blocks were delivered to the site by that fleet of "appropriate technology" vehicles.

Problems usually do have solutions. You've just got to be creative. Think "outside of the box" or, sometimes, outside of the truck and tractor. As you seek solutions to problems, always try to find the simplest, quickest and best solution.

I'm told that Thomas Edison once asked a young assistant to tell him the cubic volume of a light bulb. The young man went to work doing all sorts of complicated mathematical equations to find the answer. After a while, Mr. Edison asked him why he didn't just put the light bulb in a container of water and then measure the amount of water that was displaced—a much simpler way to find the answer.

Clarence Jordan, in his "Cotton Patch" versions of various books of the New Testament, referred to the devil as the "The Confuser." I think that's a great name for that diabolical character. God is light. God is love. God is synonymous with solutions to problems in our lives. The devil, on the other hand, is about darkness, chaos, and confusion. So, in problem solving, keep things in the light and as simple as possible.

Sometimes the solution to a problem is easy to state, but the execution is more complicated. The famous American humorist, Will Rogers, was once asked if he might have a solution to the problem of German submarines sinking Allied ships during World War I. "Yes," he replied. "I have a good solution. Just boil the ocean!"

"Boil the ocean?! How in the world could that be done?"

"I don't know," he replied. "You asked me what could be done, not how to do it!"

In 1992, when I proposed that substandard housing be eliminated in Americus and Sumter County, Georgia, by 2000, there were numerous doubters. Hundreds of families lived in shacks all over the city and county.

Many people exclaimed, "It will take millions of dollars to build or renovate houses for all of those people!"

My reply was simple: "God's got millions of dollars. It's just in the pockets of people and we've got to extract it."

An umbrella group was formed called the Sumter County Initiative. All groups and individuals in the county concerned with housing joined the Initiative. Habitat for Humanity was the guiding force, but all housing groups in the county were actively involved in the effort to eliminate poverty housing from the city and county. The Initiative was led by George Peagler, then an outstanding local attorney, now an outstanding local judge.

Construction of affordable housing in the county increased from five houses a year, all built by Habitat for Humanity, to one hundred houses a year within three years, with Habitat building half of them and other groups—the Housing Authority, Christian Rebuilders, and a private builder—doing the rest.

In September of 2000, I was able to stand in front of a house to be owned and occupied by the Thomas family and lead several hundred people singing the old gospel song, "Victory in Jesus." That house symbolized our victory over poverty housing in the city and county and is a legacy of the creative problem solving of the Sumter County Initiative.

The successful Sumter County Initiative gave birth to a program we in Habitat call the 21st Century Challenge. That pioneering venture is being led by veteran Habitat for Humanity staffer Clive Rainey. By 2002, more than 40 cities and counties in the United States had entered the program with the goal of *solving* the problem of poverty housing in their respective local areas.

In Habitat for Humanity, we are systematically and very methodically working to solve the problem of substandard and poverty housing. It's a huge task, but we are convinced that, with determination and God's blessing, it can be done!

Do you have a serious problem in your personal life or in your professional life? Are you fighting the problem or searching for a solution? Write down three possible solutions to a problem in your life. Don't forget that most problems do have solutions. Be creative and determined to find those solutions.

PERSISTENCE

Linda and I were in north Georgia at Glencove, the beautiful rustic mountain cabin on Lake Rabun (owned by our dear friends Chrys and John Street of Marietta) for a few days of vacation and for me to work on writing this book. One morning we went on a long walk down Bear Gap road, which runs in front of Glencove. The purpose of the walk was twofold. First of all, we wanted to get some exercise and, second, we wanted to get a morning newspaper from a dispenser that was about a mile and a half away.

When we got to the newspaper dispenser, we inserted two quarters and tried to open the door to retrieve our paper. The door wouldn't open. I pushed the button and the dispenser disgorged the two quarters. I reinserted the quarters. The door still wouldn't open. I pushed the button again. Out came the quarters. Linda inserted the quarters, but the door wouldn't open for her either. She pushed the button and out came one quarter. She pushed the button again and again and again. Finally, out came the second quarter. I put the money back in the dispenser, inserting each quarter with as much force as possible. The door wouldn't open. We rocked the dispenser back and forth and hit the door with our hands. Still, the door wouldn't open. I pushed the button—out came the quarters.

Well, you get the picture. The situation seemed hopeless, but we kept on putting in the quarters and pushing the button and putting in the quarters until, finally, on about the twelfth try, the door opened—and we joyfully extracted the last paper.

Persistence pays off!

You've heard the old cliché: "If at first you don't succeed, try, try again." That is such sound advice. And it's so essential to success in various endeavors in life.

The Bible teaches that "with God, all things are possible" (Matthew 19:26). The Bible does not say that all things are possible *immediately*. Neither does God's word teach that "with God, all things are easy." Some things are difficult, indeed, often incredibly difficult. As we set out to accomplish some particular task, persistence is essential and we must not grow weary as we move along.

I believe that ultimate strength comes from God. Scripture confirms that belief. Isaiah proclaims:

> God gives power to the weak. And to those who have no might He increases strength. Even the youths shall faint and be weary. And the young men shall utterly fall, but those who wait on the Lord shall renew their strength; they shall mount up with wings like eagles, they shall run and not be weary, they shall walk and not faint. (40:29)

The Bible also teaches that our persistence in life should be in doing good. And it promises that if we do not grow weary, we will experience success. The book of Galatians admonishes: "Let us not grow weary while doing good, for in due season we shall reap if we do not lose heart" (6:9).

In my life, I have known many people who were highly intelligent and very talented, but they were never able to accomplish much because they lacked focus and persistence. Such people are like the rabbit in the story of the tortoise and the hare. They could easily run ahead of the crowd because of their great talent. But, before the race is won, they stop to rest and to engage in other things. They get distracted and forget the race.

Meanwhile, the less-talented tortoise is just trudging on up the road. And guess what? The tortoise wins!

In our work with Habitat for Humanity, we have often been criticized because our approach of one house at a time is too slow and not effective to meet the great need. A massive government effort is called for. But, over time and with persistence, the slow, one-house-at-a-time approach has produced more and more houses and the numbers keep rising steadily year after year.

So, there is no substitute for persistence. If one is engaged in a pursuit and God is in it and if there is persistence and one doesn't grow weary, in due season, there will be a harvest.

Is there a situation in your life right now that calls for you to be more persistent? What steps are you taking to keep going in the face of tough obstacles?

My favorite poem is "Be Strong" by Maltbie Davenport Babcock. The last two lines of that great bit of poetry are: "Faint not. Fight on. Tomorrow comes the song." Harvest or song. Take your pick. Persistence will get either or both of them for you.

CHARACTER AND GOALS

Everyone has character. And various words describe that character. Hardworking, ambitious, humorous, loving, aggressive, methodical, studious, creative, articulate, bold, adventurous, inquisitive, and so forth.

I believe that one's character doesn't change that much as a person goes through life, but goals do change. Consider the person initially known as Saul in the New Testament. He was a religious Pharisee, strict in the interpretation and practice of the Jewish law and deeply offended by the early Christians. Saul was participating in the persecution of the Christians. He aggressively helped in trying to stamp out this "sect," which he believed was corrupting Judaism.

Then Saul had his dramatic conversion experience on the road to Damascus. He encountered Jesus and his life radically changed. He became the greatest evangelist the world has ever known. His name was changed to Paul and his goal in life changed 180 degrees from persecuting Christians to promoting the gospel of Jesus.

But his basic character did not change. The aggressive persecutor of the church became the aggressive promoter of the church. Paul was tireless in his work. He traveled constantly, planting new churches and, by correspondence and in other ways, encouraged and taught how to know and be faithful to the Lord Jesus.

Chuck Colson was an aggressive, hardworking, ambitious young lawyer who linked up with President Richard Nixon. He became embroiled in the famous Watergate scandal in the United States and ended up serving a term in prison. During that time, he was converted and became a dedicated evangelical Christian. Upon release from prison, Chuck founded Prison Fellowship, which, over the years, has become one of the best known and most admired Christian movements in the world today.

Chuck Colson's basic character did not change. He remained an aggressive, hardworking, determined man. But his goals changed. The ambitious politician became ambitious to organize and run a new program to make life better for prisoners. The man who was a cultural Christian at best became a convinced one who openly acknowledged Christ in his life and especially advocated a Christian lifestyle for men and women in prison.

Chuck Colson's redirected intelligence and energy have positively affected the lives of countless thousands of people both inside and outside of prisons all across the United States and around the world.

I have always been an energetic person. Since my youth, I have enjoyed promoting things—getting organized and making things happen. When I was a teenager, I was president of a Junior Achievement Company. We made mops and house signs. I always wanted to make more mops and signs than any other J. A. Company. And I wanted to sell the most. That excited and fulfilled me.

A few years later, at the University of Alabama, fellow student Morris Dees, Jr. and I organized a company to sell various products. He and I aggressively promoted the young company and, during our university years and in the years immediately following, the company grew to be a large operation selling millions of dollars of products and employing many people.

With the company growing dramatically, a crisis hit my life when my wife, Linda, left me, considering a divorce because we had grown apart due to my utter devotion to the young company. Out of that crisis came a change in both of us. We decided to totally change our direction in life and to seek God's path instead of pursuing wealth and more material possessions. One result of the change, of course, was Habitat for Humanity, the worldwide Christian housing ministry that is building houses with and for families in need in every state in the United States and in nearly a hundred other countries as of 2002.

My character did not change. My goals changed. I decided to use my energies and talents to promote a practical ministry that would put God's love into action to help elevate the human condition. I wanted this work to bring people together, and especially to get all churches of various denominations, Protestant and Catholic, to work together. And I wanted Linda and I to be together, united and in total agreement on an endeavor that would strengthen our relationship and be enriching to our marriage and to our whole family.

Have you done an assessment of your character? What are your strengths and weaknesses? What kinds of activities and work do you enjoy doing? What are you good at? What are your goals in life? Are those the right goals for you? Do your goals positively impact your life and the lives of others? Are they in line with God's will? Do they square up with God's word? The Bible clearly teaches that one cannot serve God and mammon (money). Which are you serving?

What, if any changes, should occur in your life? What goals should you abandon and what new goals should you adopt?

Ask God to guide you in seeking the changes that are needed in your life. Change is possible at any age and it is good if the change is in the direction of God. Use your God-given talents to pursue the new goals. You'll be blessed in the whole process. Things won't always be easy, but you will be blessed. I promise!

I encourage you to apply your character to seeking goals that serve God and the highest good of humanity and God's good earth.

FAITH

PRAYER

Mother Teresa was once asked what she did when she prayed. She responded, "I listen." Prayer does seem to have an air of mystery to it. There is so much about prayer that is hard to understand. And yet, the Bible says that we should pray without ceasing.

Jesus certainly took prayer seriously, and he prayed regularly. Throughout his earthly ministry, he often went to a lonely place to pray. When he was about to be crucified, the Bible reports that, being in agony, he prayed more earnestly and "sweat became like great drops of blood falling down to the ground" (Luke 22:44).

My spiritual mentor, Clarence Jordan, was more like Jesus than anyone I've ever known. On many occasions, I was privileged to hear him pray. Especially, I heard him pray many times before meals. His prayers were unlike any others I had ever heard. I got the strong feeling that this man was talking directly with God. He spoke in a soft, gentle voice and his prayers were penetrating and powerful. And there was a definite element of "listening" in the prayers of Clarence Jordan, even as he was speaking softly.

Clarence Jordan said that God is constantly "broadcasting." To hear what He is saying, we must extend our spiritual antennae to pick up God's messages. The receiving of God's messages is accomplished through prayer. It's that activated listening, spoken of by Mother Teresa, which is the essence of prayer.

So many people today never really listen. Their lives are perpetually filled with noise and confusion. There is simply never any time to be quiet and listen.

When our children were little, I often played the "listening game." Our routine was that I would get them to bed and then tell them either a scary story or a fairy tale. That would get them really stirred up and anything but sleepy. To calm them down, I would play the "listening game." It worked like this: The children had to lie on their backs so both ears were open and able to hear clearly. They had to be perfectly still and quiet in order to hear whatever sounds were within earshot.

Out of the quietness, someone would hear something—a car horn, a dog barking, a truck passing by, a creak in the wall, or any number of other things. When someone heard something, they would whisper, "I heard a car" or, "I heard someone talking."

Soon, everyone would be fast asleep.

The discipline of being perfectly quiet and listening, I believe, was good training for a dynamic prayer life.

I have long had the discipline of prayer in my life. I often pray, especially when I awake in the morning and at night before going to bed. Also, I usually pray before every meal, both in private and when eating in public. The prayers are often short and simple, but a definite reminder to stay in contact with the Lord God Almighty.

What does prayer accomplish? I definitely believe God hears and answers prayer. Sometimes, of course, a prayer is answered in a way that is surprising to the one praying. But, an answer is forthcoming. Prayer should seek to know God's answer—God's will—not our own. With that attitude, prayer is exciting and so deeply meaningful.

In the eleventh chapter of the Gospel of Luke, it is recorded that Jesus was praying. When he ceased, one of his disciples asked him to teach them to pray. He responded by giving them the Lord's prayer, as here recorded in the Gospel of Matthew:

Our Father in heaven,
Hallowed be your name.
Your kingdom come.
Your will be done
On earth as it is in heaven.
Give us day by day our daily bread.
And forgive our sins, for we also forgive everyone who is indebted to us.
And do not lead us into temptation,
But deliver us from the evil one. (6:9-13)

These words make it so clear that prayer should be for the purpose of discovering God's will and way. It is a humble prayer that moves us toward reverence for God, sufficiency in physical needs, forgiveness for oneself and others, and relief from temptation.

At Habitat for Humanity International headquarters, every day begins with prayer. Specific prayers are said for the sick and bereaved. We also pray for certain Habitat affiliates and campus chapters. And we pray for global work teams that serve around the world. Usually, we pray for the "denomination of the day," such as American Baptists, United Methodists, Roman Catholics, Presbyterians, and others. Above all, we pray for God to guide us in our work. Meetings held throughout the day are opened with brief prayers, again asking for God's guidance as issues are discussed and decisions made. At regional and area Habitat offices across the United States and around the world, prayers are regularly and routinely said in devotional times and to open meetings. The same is true of Habitat International board meetings and functions held by local Habitat affiliates. The annual Jimmy Carter blitz builds have devotionals each day and prayers are a central part of those devotionals.

Prayer is our connection to God. It gives us power and assurance that our activities are right and in line with what God wants us to do in our personal lives and in all other activities.

Do you have an active prayer life? Should you pray more? Perhaps a regular discipline of prayer would be beneficial to you. What do you think? I suggest that you deepen your prayer life. I believe you'll find the rewards to be quite significant and meaningful if you set aside time to sit quietly and listen to God's guidance.

THE GOD MOVEMENT

I learned about the God movement from Clarence Jordan. The God movement was Clarence's expression for the Kingdom of God. With Jesus, the Kingdom was first and foremost. He said, "Seek first the kingdom and its righteousness and all else will be added" (Matthew 6:33).

The God movement was first with Clarence too. He explained that American Christians don't really understand the concept of a "kingdom." In the United States and in most countries, there is no kingdom and there are no kings and queens and princes and princesses. But there are movements—the Civil Rights movement, the Women's Liberation movement, and so forth. The concept of a movement is understood, even in a country with a king or queen.

To Clarence, the most important thing in the world was to find out, through prayer and study, what is going on with the God movement and to become a part of it. Clarence had so immersed himself in his study of the Bible, especially the New Testament, that he literally thought like Jesus. Time and again, I would be astounded by his answers to questions and by his attitude about various subjects. He seemed to see everything from God's point of view because he was so focused on the God movement.

He once told me that every person he had studied about in the Bible, he had met in Americus and Sumter County, Georgia. I have never met another person in my life who even remotely thought about making such a linkage between contemporaries and Bible characters. I found that idea absolutely amazing.

Clarence also dealt with everyday situations within the context of the God movement. For example, he went into the town of Americus one day during the boycott (which was instituted against Koinonia Farm by the white establishment of Sumter County in an attempt to drive them from the area) and tried to purchase a sack of chicken feed. The man behind the counter flushed with anger and told him to get out of his store. As Clarence was leaving, the man yelled out to him that if he and the Koinonia people would run an advertisement in the local paper renouncing their views on integration, he would sell him anything he wanted.

Clarence stopped in his tracks and slowly walked back to the counter. "Excuse me, sir," he quietly replied, "I came in here this morning simply to buy a sack of feed. I didn't come in to sell my soul."

God was as present to Clarence as the skin on his face or the shirt on his back. That awareness of God's presence colored everything he thought about and everything he did. Of course, Clarence's thinking came straight from Jesus who taught his disciples to seek closeness to God. Seek, he said, to be a part of the Kingdom of God above all else. Clarence was that kind of a seeker. He was a devoted disciple of Jesus. His life was a great model for me. The way he thought and his practical pursuit of the God movement caused me to rethink my own faith and how I thought about God.

Perhaps you have seen the little "WWJD" bracelets—"What would Jesus do?" That is such a relevant question. If a growing number of people would seriously ask that question and respond honestly in accordance with the teachings of Jesus, the world would change quite dramatically.

In our modern world, opinion polls are ubiquitous. Politicians, especially, are so attuned to them. Decisions are made to keep in line and in tune with the opinion polls so that an office holder can stay in office or a company can maximize profits. But one who would be a part of the God movement does not look to opinion polls. He or she looks to Christ to determine a course of action.

In the days of the Freedom Riders during the Civil Rights movement, someone asked Clarence Jordan if he had ever participated in a Freedom Ride. He thought for a minute and then replied, "No, but I've always ridden freely."

What he meant was that his conduct was determined by the ideals of the God movement, not by an event such as getting a group of blacks and whites together to make a highly publicized trip.

Clarence also had a sense of humor and great wit about him in dealing with difficult situations caused by his adherence to God movement principles in the face of a contrary culture. One time he was on a trip with an African American man. His traveling companion needed to go to the rest room, but blacks were not allowed to use public toilets. Clarence walked into a service station and inquired if his "brother" could use the rest room.

"Of course," came the swift reply.

Clarence went back to the car and got his friend. The two of them walked briskly past the proprietor to the rest room. "That's a black man!" the proprietor exclaimed.

"Yes," Clarence quietly replied. "He's my brother in Christ."

They kept walking. Clarence's "brother" went in and used the rest room, came back out, and the two of them left. The proprietor was still trying to figure out what had happened!

On another occasion, Clarence entered a segregated public bus. He went to the back and sat in the section for blacks. The driver was quite agitated by this. After a few minutes, he pulled the bus over to the side of the road, got out of his seat and went back to confront Clarence.

"Sir," he sternly intoned, "You can't sit there. Please move up front to the white section."

Clarence didn't budge. "I beg your pardon, driver, I should sit here."

The driver insisted, "Mister, don't give me trouble. Get up and move!"

"Driver, I do humbly beg your pardon. You see, my mother was a white woman."

The man was visibly puzzled. "What? Okay, I beg your pardon." He went back to his seat and drove on without further comment or problem, thinking that Clarence was a light-skinned "black" man. In fact, Clarence was white with light skin and his mother was, indeed, a white woman, but his father was also white. He refused to acquiesce in what to him was an evil system of segregation and discrimination. In the tradition of Jesus, he outsmarted the driver. In the process, I imagine he helped the man see the stupidity of the system.

In any event, taking his African American friend to the rest room and sitting in the back of the bus were part of being in the God movement to Clarence Jordan. He didn't wait for some "religious" occasion or time to express his faith. Every day, every time, and any occasion were right and appropriate to express and live out God's ideas.

"What would Jesus do?" That is the question that should be asked by any serious person who would aspire to follow Christ. By doing that, you, too, will land squarely in the God movement. Being in that movement is sometimes uncomfortable, even dangerous, but always exciting and always right and pleasing to God.

I encourage you to join the God movement by living as Christ would have you live in every moment of your life.

OLD-TIME RELIGION

When I was growing up in east Alabama, a favorite church hymn was "Give Me That Old-time Religion." One refrain in the song goes, "It was good for Paul and Silas. It's good enough for me."

Over the years, I've thought about that "old-time religion." What is it? Unfortunately, I think it's about generic religion or "Brand X" Christianity. Old-time religion is about "preaching the Bible," but it doesn't relate the Bible to anything current. It keeps everything generic and in a safe, distant past.

Loving one's neighbor is just fine as long as he or she has no name and no known address. Any preacher of any denomination can preach his or her heart out about the importance of loving one's neighbor and the response will be uniformly the same—good preaching, solid theology, straight out of the Bible. It's that "old-time religion" and it doesn't threaten or challenge anyone.

But, if the preacher names a neighbor and gives not only an address but explains the needs of that neighbor, there is a problem. The parishioner has to respond in some way. One response is to run the preacher off so that such challenging preaching will no longer be heard. A new pastor or priest can be found who will stick to safe, anonymous neighbors. Another response is to quit attending church so one doesn't have to listen to such disturbing messages. One could admit that "loving one's neighbor as oneself" is merely a slogan not to be taken seriously, or one could take action to express love and practical help to the neighbor in need.

Habitat for Humanity is a vehicle that enables people, especially church people and all others of goodwill, to express love in a practical way to neighbors both near and far who need a decent place to live.

Housing is so basic to human need, and the need is universal. All families need, as a minimum, a simple, decent place to live. Helping families have a good house is a powerful and highly relevant way to demonstrate love of a neighbor. Such expressed love is new-time religion, or maybe one could say "old-time religion" better understood and applied.

I know of many churches that have Bible study groups. People will come together for years to study the Bible, but nothing ever comes of it. That is to say, the study is only for the sake of the study itself, with some fellowship thrown in. Now, I think studying is good. Increasing one's knowledge, especially of the Bible, is desirable. And fellowship is certainly a good thing. But there ought to be more than that.

To me, studying with no plan of action is like cooking great meals week after week and dumping the prepared food directly into the garbage. There is value in the work that goes into preparing a meal and, when done with others, the fellowship is likewise good. But how much better the whole process would be if the food were actually consumed, giving enjoyment and strength to those who ate it!

When one remembers that Jesus said that the essence of true faith is to love God completely and to love one's neighbor as oneself, it is prudent and wise, I think, to get serious about trying to apply that to one's daily life.

Think about the ways in which you express love to yourself. Being sure you have adequate money for food, clothing, shelter and other needs in life. Now, realize that neighbors have the same kinds of needs. Ask basic questions, such as, what kind of insurance do I have to assure that I'll be taken care of in case of illness? Is adequate insurance available for my neighbor?

True religion is practical. I don't believe in a bland sameness. People are different and their needs and aspirations are different. But all of humanity is a whole lot more similar than they are different. All need the basics—food, clothing and shelter. And, all need to feel cared for and loved . . . in practical and some not-so-practical ways.

True religion is not "Brand X" where one "loves" and cares for amorphous neighbors. True religion knows names, addresses, and needs. True religion is active and hardworking.

The world does not need "old-time religion" that is dormant and restricted to the sanctuary or to a safe, distant past. The world cries out for activated, caring religion that has on work clothes and a mind and heart to help others.

What kind of religion do you practice? Do you feel that you *really* love your neighbors as much as you love yourself? What changes need to take place in your life to cause you to be more in line with the fundamental teaching that you should love a neighbor as much as you love yourself?

Challenge yourself to make old-time religion new through expressions of love and service.

RELEVANT RELIGION

One Sunday morning, I was getting ready to go to Sunday school and church. Part of my preparation was to read over the lesson in the Sunday school book. I was delighted to see that the topic for that day was "Race Relations." My delight, however, turned to dismay as I discovered that the heart of the lesson was on how to get along with Cambodians.

I wondered where the writer of the lesson lived because, in south Georgia, there are very few Cambodians. Furthermore, across the United States, while there are Cambodians in some communities, they are a small percentage of the population. I thought, perhaps, that the writer lived in an area with a substantial Cambodian population and that there was a local problem in relations with them. To my surprise, I learned from a section in the lesson book on the author that he lived in Texas. I thought the Cambodian population was about the same there as in Georgia—very, very low.

I wrote to the author and asked why in a lesson on "race relations" he wrote about how to get along with Cambodians. I asked the pointed question: "Why didn't you write about the black-white race relations problem?" "That," I said, "is the *relevant* race relations problem in the United States."

In his reply back to me, the author said that he thought the black-white issue was too volatile, so he decided to choose an approach that would not engender a hostile reaction. In other words, he decided to be irrelevant. Unfortunately, that approach of irrelevance is all too common in many churches.

Clarence Jordan at Koinonia Farm decided to be relevant in his approach to living out his Christian faith. Although very controversial in the 1940s and 1950s, he and others who lived at Koinonia dealt head-on with the race issue. African Americans were accepted and treated with respect and as equals.

Such behavior enraged the local white power structure, but Clarence stood his ground. He also espoused nonviolence and nonmaterialism in a militaristic and materialistic society.

To make sure no one misunderstood his position on race relations, Clarence published his "Cotton Patch" versions of certain sections of the New Testament. He had Jesus living in Georgia, dealing with blacks and whites instead of Jews and Samaritans.

In his "Cotton Patch" gospels, the Good Samaritan (an African American) passes through Ellaville, just north of Americus. He sees a white man who has been beaten up there. The victim is on the side of the highway, obviously in a serious condition. A white revival preacher has already passed him by and, likewise, a white gospel singer. The African American, though, stops and binds up the wounds of the man and takes him to the hospital.

Such a retelling and recasting of a familiar Bible story was anathema to local whites. They loved the Good Samaritan doing his good deed two thousand years ago on a lonely road between Jerusalem and Jericho. But don't put that guy on my highway between Atlanta and Albany. That's where I live! And, for sure, don't change his race and make him black! That's unacceptable.

But Clarence Jordan was in the great tradition of Jesus in recasting stories to make them relevant. Jesus didn't get nailed to a cross for carrying little lambs around in his arms. He healed and picked grain on the Sabbath. He threw the moneychangers out of the temple. He allowed a woman of bad reputation to wash his feet with her tears and dry them with her hair. He ate with despised tax collectors. He lambasted the respected religious leaders of his day for their hypocrisy. And, of course, the ultimate insult was to proclaim that he was God's own son.

His religion was powerful and relevant. It was full of salt and yeast and light.

To me, the challenge of Clarence Jordan and, to a much greater extent, the challenge of Jesus, is to be relevant in our proclamation and practice of what we believe.

The ministry of house-building at Koinonia, initially called Partnership Housing and which evolved into Habitat for Humanity, was an attempt to be relevant in our understanding of God's word. The Bible teaches plainly that we should express God's love and that such love should be expressed in tangible ways, such as feeding the hungry, clothing the naked, housing the homeless (invite strangers in), and so forth.

We were painfully aware of the lack of adequate housing all around us in south Georgia in the late 1960s. So we launched a house-building ministry by building one house for a family in need.

As neighbors learned about what we were doing and they found out that we were planning to sell the houses at no profit and no interest, they scoffed at the whole idea, saying that it was un-American and sounded communistic. We responded that the idea came from the Bible. Their comeback was that the Bible is okay, but for Sunday school and church. The concept of doing business with an idea from the Bible seemed radical and unrealistic.

Radical? Maybe. But needed and definitely relevant.

The relevant application of the ancient principle of not attempting to profit from the poor, wedded to the ageless concept of loving one's neighbor as oneself, expressed through building simple, decent houses for and with families in need, has produced a growing movement around the world. Habitat for Humanity, operating as a Christian ministry that draws together all of the various denominations—liberal and conservative, Protestant and Catholic, including all races and open to all people, Christian or not—to serve and contribute and to receive houses, this little mustard-seed size expression of relevant religion is expanding exponentially around the world.

Relevant religion has power. Full of God's love, it can transform the world.

How can you make your beliefs more relevant in today's world? What changes need to be made in the practice of your faith to make it relevant and more pertinent to all aspects of your life and to all of your various relationships, both personal and in regard to your community, state, nation, and world?

I encourage you to live your faith by choosing to be relevant in today's world.

WORSHIP

God is Spirit and those who worship Him must worship in spirit and truth. (John 4:24)

When we contemplate God, there is mystery. No one has ever seen God. We have ideas about God. Millions upon millions of words have been written about God. We even have many names for God: Yahweh, Lord, Father, Creator, Allah, and on and on. No matter how long we think and no matter how many books we read and regardless of how many sermons we have listened to, there is still mystery. We see and understand God only in small part.

The Bible says that God is Spirit. You cannot see a spirit. But we have every confidence it is there. One cannot see gravity or radio beams or a magnetic field, but those things are there.

Since God is Spirit, we must worship in spirit and, the Bible admonishes, also in truth. What does that mean? To me it requires a cleansing of the mind. To prepare for a worship experience, whether in a church sanctuary or on top of some lonely mountain, a person who would worship God must clear all extraneous matter from his or her mind and open a pathway into the mind, heart, and soul so that the spirit can flow into us. In the process of clearing away extraneous matter, the most essential thing to remove is all elements of falsehood. After all, God is Spirit. That Spirit knows no barriers of any kind. It permeates the most remote recesses of our being. Nothing can be hidden or unknown to this free-flowing Spirit. Realizing that, we can be completely open to God. Communication takes place and something happens. We are changed, or we are ready for change.

Sometimes, I think, public worship is an impediment to true worship. People arrive at church, laughing and joking. They are very concerned about what others are wearing. Gossip flows freely. Loud talking continues right up to the moment the church service begins. I wonder if there is a conscious effort to reflect on God and His awesome presence? I wonder if there is a desire on the part of the worshippers to strip away falsehood and open a clear channel for God to flow into their lives?

I do believe public worship is important. When I was growing up, we went to church every Sunday. There was never a discussion about whether or not to go to church. That would have been like discussing whether or not to eat.

Throughout my life, I've tried to attend worship regularly. In more recent years, I've traveled extensively so I am often away from home. Even so, on the road I am usually in church on Sunday, most often as a speaker or preacher of the day.

A person who has impressed me with his faithful church attendance is former President Carter. He has a lifetime habit of regularly attending church, even when he is away from home. And having been in church with him and his wife, Rosalynn, on numerous occasions, I've noticed that the two of them are quiet and reverent, both before and during the service. I have always sensed that they are very conscientious about worshipping God in spirit and in truth.

Many people say they don't need to attend church to worship God. Maybe that is true, but there is importance in a routine where one *regularly* worships God. Attending church Sunday after Sunday, it seems to me, has value. Also, I believe there is strength in being with fellow believers. There is a certain synergy to the assembled congregation, focusing together on God and on His majesty and power.

Worship is not a panacea. It is not the sum total of our duty as believers. Jesus did not say, for example, "The first and great commandment is this, 'Thou shall go to church.'" The Bible does teach that we should not forsake the assembling of ourselves together. But that assembling is to worship, to reflect on God, to listen to a message and be strengthened, to be light, salt, and leaven in the world, making a difference and being a part of God's activity that helps to usher in the Kingdom of God on earth.

Do you regularly attend church? If so, is it a fulfilling spiritual experience? Are there any changes that should be made in the way you worship? Or, should you consider changing where you worship? If you do not regularly attend worship, do you think seeking a place of worship would add a spiritual dimension to your life?

Make a list of reasons why you do not attend church regularly, as well as a list of the benefits that regular worship could provide you.

SALVATION

In the culture in which I was raised, in the Deep South of the United States, I was surrounded by Protestant Christians. I knew only a few Catholics and even fewer Jews. I was an adult before I met my first Muslim, Hindu, and Buddhist.

The teaching that was implanted in my mind and heart at home, in the community, and at church was that salvation comes from God, through Christ, by his sacrifice on the cross at Calvary. I accepted that teaching and that understanding of God. I was baptized and became a professing Christian. As a matter of faith, I embraced what I had been taught. I believed as a child and I believe now that Jesus of Nazareth was and is the Son of God who suffered and died on a cross for my sins. I believe he was crucified and buried and that, on the third day, he rose from the grave and now resides in Heaven with God the Heavenly Father.

I passionately believe what I believe. I consider myself a *convinced* Christian and not simply a *cultural* one. But I have come to realize that what I believe is just that, *belief*. I don't *know* any of the above, but I do deeply *believe* it. Others passionately believe something different.

When I was a teenager, I met a wonderful young woman named Leah. I was very fond of her. She was intelligent, attractive, and a lot of fun. She was also Jewish.

I became deeply concerned about her because I felt that if she died without accepting Christ, she would go to hell. I didn't want that for Leah, but I didn't know how to get her to join my church or some other church, be baptized, and thus be saved from eternal damnation.

I never got any peace about that matter until I met Clarence Jordan. He helped me understand, for the first time in my life, that salvation comes from God and not from me or any other person. Hence, I should simply say, or witness, to what I believe, and leave redemptive activity to God. God loves Leah and His love is not dependent on any activity or inactivity on her part. Furthermore, His love is forever and will extend throughout her life on earth and into the next life.

St. Paul said that we now "see darkly, but eventually [after death] face to face and clearly" (1 Corinthians 13:12). All truth will ultimately be revealed by God.

That insight was incredibly liberating to me. It allowed me to be free as a convinced Christian to express what I believe to whomever and, more importantly, to love everybody, regardless of their profession of faith, or no faith, and leave redemption to God.

Muslims believe salvation comes from God and that Mohammed is his prophet. There are cultural Muslims, just as there are cultural Christians. I remember a story I once heard about a young man who became a Christian, was baptized, and joined a church. Soon thereafter, he planned to go on a trip with several of his friends, none of whom were Christian. The young man went to his pastor for advice. The pastor told him to simply be faithful to his new life in Christ and to be in prayer along the way. When the trip was over the young man went back to see his pastor. He was excited, "Good news, pastor. I had no trouble on the trip. My friends never found out I was a Christian."

A similar story was told to me by a Christian about an encounter with a Muslim. The two of them became friends at a place where they were employed. The Christian man invited the Muslim to his home for dinner. The Muslim accepted the invitation. A few days later, the Christian began to wonder if the Muslim perhaps had some dietary restrictions because of his religion. He asked him. The Muslim replied, "Don't worry about that. I never allow my religion to interfere with anything I want to do."

But there are convinced Muslims, countless thousands of them. They passionately believe what they believe, just as I do and as countless other Christians do. The same is true of other religions. Some people are cultural Jews, Hindus, and Buddhists, and others passionately believe the basic tenets of their religion. They are absolutely convinced of the correctness of their belief.

There are many things that disturb me about my country, but one thing that I am so proud of is freedom of religion, a hallmark of the United States. People are free to be passionate about whatever they believe, as long as the practice of their religion does not infringe on the rights and freedom of others.

I believe evangelists of whatever persuasion should be free to try to convince others of the truth of their beliefs in all countries. But love should be proclaimed and never hatred. Never should there be any element of coercion. Likewise, the understanding that salvation ultimately comes from God should be implicit and explicit in every conversation.

Problems arise when a person or a group of people take it upon themselves to be God's holy appointed ones. They *know* God's truth and it is their *duty* to make sure their understanding of truth prevails. All who disagree are enemies of God and worthy only of ridicule, persecution, and death.

That despicable attitude is avoided if there is the simple understanding that salvation comes from God. God is love. Love is eternal, extending forever, everywhere and to everyone. And, if I love God and God is love, I should also love and love without limits.

Persuading humanity to embrace the above would stop the endless cycle of war and hatred that has been the lot of humanity for thousands of years.

METANOIA

You must be born again.

As a southern Protestant, I've heard that refrain all my life. It's what Jesus told Nicodemus he must do to inherit eternal life. Nicodemus was confused by the statement and many people today are still in a quandary as to what it means.

When Jimmy Carter was running for president for the first time in the 1970s, he said he was a "born-again" Christian. Questions abounded across the land. "What does *that* mean?"

In evangelical circles the world over, the outward sign of being "born again" is accepting Christ as Lord and Savior, being baptized, and joining a church. The theological concept is that everyone has an earthly father, but to become a "citizen of Heaven," one must have God as a father. When a person submits to God and God comes into the life of that person, he or she then has God as a new father, a Heavenly father, and a new creature comes into existence. The birth that results from a "refathering" by God produces a "child of God." A person has been "born again."

Clarence Jordan, founder of the Christian community of Koinonia Farm in southwest Georgia and celebrated author of the "Cotton Patch" version of the New Testament, had some profound insights into this whole subject of being "born again." He reasoned that many people are "born again," but God, the Heavenly Father, is not the father in the rebirthing. Clarence pointed out that the church is the "vehicle" or "womb" of God in the rebirthing process. The Bible makes it clear that the church is the "Bride of Christ" and that bride should produce children of God.

What happens, though, is that so often the church has other lovers, the principal one of which is "mammon" (material things such as money, big buildings, fancy ornaments, and so forth.) The church becomes enamored of all those new "lovers" and God, the Heavenly Father, gets shoved aside.

Clarence often called churches "God boxes." He said people get together, organize a "church," and proceed to define the kind of God they want to reside in their "God box." In the south, especially, one of the criteria for a "God box" is that only people of a certain race or economic status are welcome. The God of that church must only bless those certain people who are acceptable to be in that particular "God box." Clarence said, "Guess what? The Lord of the universe, the God who created all of humanity, doesn't show up!" And the people who are "born again" in the womb of that "God box" do not have God the Heavenly Father as their "daddy."

Clarence went on to explain that an authentic rebirthing with God, the heavenly Father, as the true Father, is by a process called *metanoia*.

Metanoia is a Greek word. Our English word "metamorphosis" comes from *metanoia*, which means transformation, a total and complete change. It is what happens when a caterpillar goes through its dramatic change to become a butterfly. The little fuzzy caterpillar crawls around on the ground and up on a weed or grass stem. Then, one day, it attaches itself to a twig and goes into a dormant stage called a cocoon. The forces of nature go to work and an amazing change takes place. Some time later the cocoon breaks open and a butterfly emerges. It doesn't even remotely resemble the caterpillar. The caterpillar, ugly and earthbound, has become a beautiful creature that can fly and go where it will, freed from the restrictions of a slow-moving, earthbound existence. The butterfly can soar up into the sky and seek out fragrant flowers, alight on them, extend its long proboscis, and extract delicious nectar.

Clarence said that an authentic conversion or "born-again" experience is like that. When God is our Father, a total transformation takes place. We are no longer "earthbound," crawling around in an earthly sinful state. Instead, we are liberated from the earth. We are free to soar in the heavens with God and His angels.

Clarence pointed out that when Jesus launched his ministry he exclaimed, "Repent, for the Kingdom of Heaven is at hand" (Matthew 4:17). The English translation of what Jesus said loses the power of what he was communicating. "Repentance," in English, has a certain element of feeling sorry for getting caught. That is not what Jesus was saying. The original Greek for what Jesus said is this, "Metanoeite, ēngiken qar hē basileia tōn ouranōn." "Change your whole way of thinking, for God's new order of the spirit is confronting you and challenging you."

Such a transformed person is a true child of God. And such a person, with God as a Father, no longer sees the world through the eyes of a white or black person, a wealthy or poor person, an American, French, or Korean person. Rather, a child of God sees and relates to the world through the inclusive, accepting, understanding, and loving eyes of God.

Have you been "born again"? That is to say, have you allowed God to transform your life as your Heavenly Father? If not, why not? I believe it's the most important decision you'll ever make.

Free yourself from an earthbound existence through the transformation of *metanoia*.

YOUR CALLING

Are you doing with your life what God put you on the earth to do? I believe that there is a certain way of living and working that is right for every person. I believe fervently that God created each person "in His own image" and for a certain kind of life and life's work.

It is your *calling*. Some people are fortunate to have found their calling. Others seem to have missed it. Have you ever heard someone exclaim, "You've missed your calling"? Usually, that expression is made to a person who has just given a good devotional talk. "You've missed your calling. You should have been a preacher!"

Some parents have preconceived notions about what their children should do with their lives. Perhaps a loving father has a successful business or law or dental practice. He decides that his beloved son should take over the business or join the law firm or dental practice. The only problem is that the son has no inclination or desire along those lines. But pressure is placed on the child and he goes along with dad's plan. The result is a frustrated person because he is not pursuing his calling. He is following his father's plan for him.

I once knew a young lawyer who went into that field of study because his parents pushed him in that direction. He gave in to the pressure. He was a reasonably good lawyer, but not at all happy in his practice. It was not until he got out of the law practice that he found deeper meaning in his new life of being a builder.

Can you know what your calling is? I certainly think so. But you must seek in order to discover that. Dr. Martin Luther King, Jr. spoke about this matter. He said simply, "Set yourself earnestly to discover what you are made to do, and then give yourself passionately to the doing of it."

I have a dear friend in Tupelo, Mississippi, whose name is Luther Millsaps. He has many wonderful expressions. One of them is this, "What melts your butter?" In other words, what is of enormous interest to you? What is your passion? What excites you and makes you glad you're alive? What makes you wake up in the morning with a great desire to get your breakfast and get going on that something that really moves and motivates you?

That something is your calling. Often it is missed because we are programmed to believe that a certain lifestyle is essential to happiness. So we pursue something that produces dollars but no meaning and no joy. Or, inertia keeps us from making a change to get our lives in line with our true purpose.

I well remember a conversation I had one time with an elderly woman who was reminiscing about her husband and his life's work. He had operated an appliance store for most of his adult life. "He shouldn't have been in that business," she sadly related. "He never enjoyed it." But, for whatever reason, he never made a move to change. Finally, he retired early to get away from something that gave him no joy or meaning. For the rest of his life, he and his wife just rode around in a recreational vehicle on a perpetual vacation, mostly fishing and camping, from Alaska to Florida. He also managed his investments. Those activities, she said, he really enjoyed.

Another retired friend told me how he wanted to be a farmer. When he was growing up, however, farming was considered a last resort career option. There was no money in farming so he opted to go into a law career. He had a very successful career as a lawyer, but his heart was always into growing things. When he retired, he started gardening. It has brought him enormous satisfaction and happiness. When he talks about the things he grows in his garden, he is totally animated and his face radiates excitement and joy.

In my life, I started out in high school engaged in a youth program called Junior Achievement. That work was meaningful to me. I enjoyed the challenge of producing a product and then promoting and selling it. I was also engaged in a youth program in my church denomination. I liked that. It involved organizing meetings and going on speaking trips to motivate young people in their Christian life and to be active in the youth program of the church.

At the same time, my father had a farm and I enjoyed the outdoor activities of working on the farm, which included plowing, mending fences, taking care of cattle, and so forth. My father also owned and operated a grocery store and soft ice cream business. I hated working in those businesses. I decided as a teenager that I never wanted to own or operate either a grocery store or a restaurant.

As I prepared for college, I decided to pursue a degree in Agricultural Engineering. I followed that course of study for a year before deciding it wasn't for me. It was not my calling. So I changed courses and ended up with a major in economics and a minor in mathematics and physics. But I had no clear sense of calling.

I got involved in student politics and enjoyed that but didn't know if it should be my career. On a whim, I took the law school admission test and made a good grade. I decided to go to law school. In law school I met a fellow student named Morris Dees, Jr., and the two of us decided to be law and business partners. We were together for eight years.

Then, a crisis in my marriage resulted in a drastic change in the direction of my life. I opened myself up to God's leading and the result has been a magnificent journey. My work with Habitat for Humanity has, over the years, utilized all of my interests and abilities. As president of Habitat for Humanity International, I organize, plan, promote, speak widely, write articles and books, get involved in legal matters, and help develop and expand a worldwide faith-inspired movement. I fervently believe this work is what God put me on this earth to do. It's what I feel called to do with my life. I am blessed and so fortunate.

The Bible speaks often about a calling to do God's work. Jesus called all of His disciples to join Him in His great work of proclaiming the kingdom of God on earth. Happy and wise, I think, is the person who responds to God's call. The book of Romans promises that "all things work together for good to those who love God, to those who are called according to His purpose" (8:28).

So listen to God's call. Assess your interests and abilities. Think about your unique talents and how God wants you to use those talents. Then, with Isaiah of old, respond humbly and simply, "Here am I. Send me." Go wherever to fulfill your calling in life. That may mean stepping across the hall. It may mean staying right where you are. Or, it could mean going back to school, moving to another state or to another country on the other side of the world. But, if you get in harmony with why you were created, you are in for a joyful time.

CHALLENGES

LEARNING FROM FAILURE

Life is a series of successes, failures, and "not sures." We should learn from every experience in life, but I believe that we often learn more from failure than we do from success. When we fail, there is a necessity to thoroughly evaluate everything, to examine all aspects of the situation to discover what went wrong and why. That process teaches a lot if we are open to learning.

One of my most painful personal failures was at Auburn University in Alabama. As an undergraduate student, I got involved in student affairs, including writing a column for the school newspaper. In the process of writing that column and as a result of other activities, I learned that there was only one political party on campus. It was called the "All Campus" party and was controlled by the sororities and fraternities. These Greek organizations would put up a slate of officers for student government and they would be routinely elected without opposition.

A group of us thought this was wrong, so we formed a rival political party called the "War Eagle" party. In the next election, we would offer our slate of officers to challenge the "in" crowd. Our support would come from the independent students. The head count clearly showed that we should win. Independent students far outnumbered members of the sororities and fraternities.

I was nominated and selected to be the candidate for president of the student body on the "War Eagle" ticket and the campaign swung into high gear. I recruited the many foreign students on campus to support me. I spoke at various meetings all over campus. I even had some little jackets made for the many dogs that roamed the campus. On both sides of those jackets were printed in bold white letters, "Fuller for President." Literally hundreds of people assured me that I would not only win, but I would win in a landslide. I believed them.

On election night I went to bed absolutely convinced I would be the next president of the student body. But, to my horror, I learned the next morning that I had narrowly lost. I was devastated. I felt rejected, a failure, and worthless as a human being. I cannot adequately describe how terrible I felt.

As I recovered over the next several days, I analyzed the whole matter. Here is what I learned. People will tell you what they know you want to hear. An election is not nearly so important to the average voter as it is to the candidate. Winning "on paper" is not the same as actually winning. Having the larger constituency doesn't necessarily mean you will win. Good intentions don't count in an election; it's only those who *actually* vote who determine the election outcome. Finally, and perhaps most important of all, I learned that life goes on after losing an election.

Another spectacular failure came a year later when I was a freshman student at the University of Alabama law school. A fellow student and I decided to launch a business venture to sell mistletoe during the Christmas season. Mistletoe grew in great abundance in the many large trees on campus. We got the bright idea of marketing the mistletoe by mail to florists in northern states. We designed and printed a colorful brochure offering beautiful "southern mistletoe—40 cents a pound." Several hundred of the brochures were mailed to florists in New York, Pennsylvania, Ohio, and other northern states.

Within days, we had orders for more than 3,000 pounds of mistletoe! We were ecstatic. Everything we made on the sale, except for small shipping expenses, would be profit. We were already counting up how much we would make. For two poor students, it was a lot.

The only problem was getting the mistletoe out of the trees. When we started going around campus with big baskets to gather the mistletoe, we discovered that it was higher than we had remembered. None of the mistletoe was on low-hanging limbs.

We got some long cane poles to try to knock the mistletoe down. Hitting the mistletoe with the poles, though, smashed the leaves and the beautiful little white berries. We realized that our customers would not be happy with that smashed-up mistletoe.

So we got rifles and started trying to shoot the mistletoe to make it fall. That didn't work because the bullets would just go right through the stems and nothing would fall.

Finally, after hours of work, we had a pile of mistletoe about three feet high. We weighed it. One pound! At that point, we realized that our great idea wasn't so great after all. We had to write all of our customers and explain that their customers would not be kissing under our mistletoe because we couldn't deliver what we had promised.

But we learned a lot from that humorous failure. First, and most important, we learned that we could get orders—and many of them—through the mail. We just had to find another product. We also learned that research was so essential to the success of a venture. We found out that what appears to be a certain reality may not actually be the situation.

The next product we offered for sale was imported Italian holly wreaths. Initially, we sold them through the Boy Scouts in the university town of Tuscaloosa and, the following year, through Hi-Y and Tri-Hi-Y clubs of the YMCA all across the country. Other products were added and, over the next eight years, our little company grew to employ more than a hundred people and sales were in the millions of dollars. And it all started from a failure.

I subsequently left business to seek God's path for my life. That quest led to the eventual founding of Habitat for Humanity. We have had many successes in the work of Habitat but some notable failures, too. I recall one idea that failed, but it produced something even better.

Several years ago I came up with the idea of building a whole town in a week. The idea was to go into a small town in a place like Mississippi and organize a big work team to build or renovate a house for every family in need in the entire city.

Former President Carter was already involved with us at that point, so we would get him to work with a big workforce. For a variety of reasons, the idea fizzled, but what emerged instead is the annual Jimmy Carter Work Project, which has now built many hundreds of houses over the past eighteen years and has inspired the building of thousands more. Also, the program to end substandard housing in our local area of Americus and Sumter County, Georgia, proved to be a huge success. It took eight years to accomplish the goal, but that successful effort gave birth to the 21st Century Challenge, which is now inspiring scores of towns and cities to set an actual date to end poverty housing.

The Bible teaches that love never fails, but it seems that love is just about the only thing that has a zero failure rate. Even faith itself sometimes fails. Jesus prayed for Peter's faith not to fail (see Luke 22:32), but Peter's faith did fail. He denied Jesus three times when he was tested. But from that ignominious failure, Peter rose to become one of the greatest saints of the Bible and the rock on which the church of Jesus Christ was built.

So failure need not be the final chapter.

Have you suffered a failure lately? What did you learn from it? How can that failure serve you to enable greater achievements in the future?

Write down three lessons you learned from a failure in your life and how those lessons can help you in the future.

It is possible to learn from the teacher called failure and go on to greater things. Why not turn your failures into your life's greatest successes?

OVERCOMING DOUBT

Everyone has doubts. Nagging doubts. Lingering doubts. Doubts about yourself. Doubts about others. Doubts about what you believe or have trouble believing about God.

When I graduated from law school, I opened a law office with my partner in Montgomery, Alabama. For two years we practiced law, along with operating a growing direct mail/publishing business. As the business grew, our law practice diminished. Eventually, we took down our law shingle and stopped practicing law altogether.

For the next three years, I worked full-time in business activities. Then Linda and I left business and moved to New York, where I worked in development work for Tougaloo, an African American college in Mississippi. I also traveled extensively on weekends, speaking on behalf of missionary work for the foreign mission board of our church denomination. The work for Tougaloo and the foreign mission board lasted for nearly three years.

From New York, we moved to Georgia to live and work at Koinonia Farm near Americus. That's where the partnership housing program was launched.

After nearly four years at Koinonia and a ten-year hiatus from practicing law, I decided to pursue admission to the Georgia Bar. Linda and I had four children, and I knew it would be expensive to educate them. Also, I was getting more concerned about certain situations in the county where we lived that could possibly be improved by a lawyer with a social conscience.

There was a problem. Admission to the Georgia Bar required passing a rigorous two-day examination, and I had learned that it was one of the toughest in the nation.

Could I pass the test? I had doubts.

I learned about a three-week intensive course at the University of Georgia to help prepare for the test. I enrolled and, full of doubt and fear, I listened and studied intently. When I took the test at the end of the course, I passed.

I was ready to practice law in Georgia. But first, Linda and I decided to do a three-year missionary assignment in Africa. That's when we launched the "housing project" in Mbandaka, the capital city of Equator Region, Zaire, and in Ntondo, a village ninety miles to the south.

When we returned from Africa, I opened a law office in Americus and one room of that building was the first office of Habitat for Humanity. I had no law books and no clients. I was besieged with doubts about whether I could make a success of my law practice, but I was determined.

My first client was a man charged with vehicular homicide. I worked day and night to prepare the case. I well remember going into court to pick a jury for the case. When I proceeded to qualify the prospective jurors, I got all kinds of strange stares from the other lawyers in the courtroom. Even the judge was surprised at how I was asking the questions.

Eventually, a recess was called and the judge summoned me to the bench. "Why are you questioning the jurors the way you are?"

"I'm following the statute, your Honor."

I showed the judge the pertinent section in the statute book. After he read through the section, he had to agree that I was following the law. But he told me, "We don't do it like that down here." The district attorney didn't follow the law on some matters either.

My doubts and fear had motivated me to prepare thoroughly. I won the case and began to establish my reputation as a lawyer.

My next case was a civil one. Again, I had doubts. I was all alone in the courtroom against lawyers who had tried cases like this one for years. Again, though, I prepared thoroughly and won that case.

Doubt can be paralyzing and negative, but healthy doubt can motivate one to strive hard and do the extra work that will bring about a good and desired result.

In addition to self-doubt, there is often doubt about others—doubt about a spouse, friend, or business associate. Something happens. Suspicion is aroused and a relationship falls into jeopardy. Sometimes, of course, doubt is justified. A doubt might turn out to be pretty much that which was suspected in the first place.

On the other hand, doubt sometimes sours a relationship for no legitimate reason.

I don't think there is a magical formula for dealing with doubt toward another person. I do think it is good to talk directly and openly with the person you have doubt about to get things cleared up between you. Unresolved doubt, whether in a business, friendship, marriage, or other relationship, is detrimental to that relationship.

The most serious doubt, of course, is in the matter of faith. I daresay that everyone has doubts of some kind concerning faith at one time or another.

The greatest doubter of all, of course, was Jesus' disciple, Thomas. His doubting about the resurrection of Jesus gave the world the expression "Doubting Thomas." He could not believe that Jesus had risen from the dead until he put his hands in the hands of Jesus and felt the gashes caused by the nails that riveted Jesus to the cross.

Earlier in Jesus' ministry, a man went to Jesus to ask healing for his son. Jesus told the man, "If you can believe, all things are possible to him who believes." In response, the man cried out, "Lord, I believe, help my unbelief!" (Mark 9:23-24). This man's cry is that of so many people who want to believe and yet doubt remains.

Peter was such a man. Jesus walked on the water. Peter wanted to do the same, so Jesus said, "Come!" Peter stepped out and began to walk on the water toward Jesus. But the wind was boisterous and Peter got scared. He began to sink. "Lord, save me!" he cried out. Jesus stretched out his hand and caught him. As Jesus pulled Peter to safety, he exclaimed, "O you of little faith, why did you doubt?" (Matthew 8:26).

Why did Peter doubt? The Bible says "the wind was boisterous." He got scared. Peter was doing something that was incredible, far out of the ordinary. He succeeded by walking in faith for a few moments, but then the wind got to him. He was frightened and he focused on his fear and doubt rather than Jesus. He began to sink.

Scripture promises the great rewards of faith. What do you desire? Wisdom or something else good from God? Ask in faith and you will receive. The book of James tells us how to ask, and it also issues a stern warning about the perils of doubting: "Ask in faith, with no doubting, for he who doubts is like a wave of the sea driven and tossed by the wind. For let not that man suppose that he will receive anything from the Lord; he is a double-minded man, unstable in all his ways" (1:6-8).

"I believe; help my unbelief" is truly one of the great and most honest prayers in the Bible. I think that prayer should be on the lips of anyone who is struggling with doubt. Faith is a leap. It's "walking on the water" of life. It cannot be done alone and it cannot be done if one is full of fear.

Pray for faith. Pray for freedom from doubt and disbelief. Faith is the better way. It is the only way, I believe, that leads to life.

FACING FEARS

At one time or another, almost everyone is gripped with fear. A bump in the night awakens us and we are afraid that someone is breaking into the house. A neighbor threatens dire action because of some real or imagined slight or hurt. A terrorist attack leaves us feeling vulnerable and our hearts are frozen with fear. The unexpected happens, and fear invades every fiber of our being. How do we deal with it?

Several times in my life, I have experienced gut-wrenching fear. When Martin Luther King, Jr. led the march from Selma to Montgomery, Linda and I hosted some of the marchers in our home in Montgomery. We received death threats. Sleep was difficult. Fear invaded every aspect of our lives. More recently, a man in Americus threatened to kill me. He didn't have anything against me. He didn't even know me. He just wanted to die. He decided that killing someone fairly prominent would surely get him the death penalty. I was tipped off by a woman who overheard a conversation about his intention, and the killing was averted by prompt, professional police work. (Unfortunately, when the man was released from jail a few years later, he gunned down a couple in a nearby parking lot. He didn't know either of them. I testified at his trial in a futile attempt to save him from a death sentence. He awaits his date with a state-imposed death sentence as this book is being written.)

Clarence Jordan and others at Koinonia had plenty of experience with fear. They were subjected to shootings, burnings, bombings, and beatings because of their witness against racism and discrimination in the segregated South of the 1940s and 50s. The people of Koinonia were harassed and persecuted for years because the members of the community refused to abide by the customs of the day in racial matters. Bullets from night riders would often rip through their houses, waking up everybody and filling the residents with fear. When Koinonia people went to town in nearby Americus, they would be cursed, threatened, and, on occasion, beaten.

So Clarence Jordan had abundant experience with fear. He also had keen insights into how to deal with it. He said that fear is good in the sense that it helps us to preserve life. Our adrenaline flows stronger and faster. Our senses are awakened and put on highest alert. But fear can also have a paralyzing effect. You've heard the expression "frozen with fear." We can become immobilized. A healthy dose of fear helps preserve our life; too much fear demoralizes and stops us from functioning in our daily lives. Or, it can cause us to be diverted from some activity that we really believe in. To me, that is not a good or right response to fear.

Clarence said that faith and fear, like light and dark, are opposites. The more fear one has, the less room there is for faith. Conversely, the more faith one has, the less room there is for fear. Fear, Clarence went on to say, is the polio of the soul, which prevents our walking by faith.

These simple insights of Clarence Jordan have been a source of enormous strength to me. I hope they are to you, too.

Fear should be kept in perspective. It shouldn't keep us from functioning. It should be faced, not run away from. It should be overcome by faith and by a resolute determination not to allow this God-given emotion to become a tool of timidity and darkness.

Some fears, of course, are not external. A common fear is the fear of failure. Many people hold back from attempting certain things because they are afraid of failing.

One fear experienced by a great many people is the fear of a health problem. A pain suddenly develops in the abdomen or some other part of the body. What is it? Do I have cancer or heart trouble or some other dreaded disease? Will I become disabled? What's going to become of me? Am I going to die? Fear grips the heart and soul with a mighty hold.

Another common fear is that of rejection. Approaching another person is often avoided because of this fear of rejection. And even the fear of rejection by God sometimes holds a person back from exploring that relationship because the person feels inadequate or unworthy.

Do you have fear in your life? How are you dealing with it? Are you "frozen or paralyzed by fear," or are you squarely facing your fears and overcoming them with faith?

Whatever fears you have, I encourage you to face them squarely. Fill your life so full of faith that there is no room left for paralyzing fear.

RELEASING REVENGE

Is it ever appropriate to seek revenge?

What about a situation where an individual or a group of people do something particularly horrible, such as the terrorist attack of September 11, 2001?

I recall seeing a huge picture on the front page of a newspaper on the morning after the United States started bombing Afghanistan following the September 11 attack. A group of young men were holding up a big banner that read simply, "REVENGE!"

All over the United States in the aftermath of the attack, people enthusiastically sang "God Bless America." So it is clear that the people of this country highly desired God's blessings upon us. But should a "God-blessed country" seek revenge?

There is support in Scripture for the government to take action against wrongdoers. Chapter 13 of Romans reads, "Rulers are not a terror to good works, but to evil . . . for he is God's minister to you for good. But if you do evil, be afraid; for he does not bear the sword in vain; for he is God's minister, an avenger to execute wrath on him who practices evil" (vv. 3-4).

But individuals and governments alike should always act with restraint and in proportion to the evil act in question. Unbridled reaction to evil with a red-hot heart of revenge is wrong. Immediately after the September 11 attack, a United States senator said, "I say bomb the hell out of them. If there's collateral damage, so be it. They certainly found our civilians to be expendable." The clear import of that statement is that it is okay to kill innocent people since "they" killed innocent people. There is no support in the Bible for that kind of irresponsible response.

What the senator said was very popular with many people because he articulated what they were thinking and feeling. Revenge is a visceral thing. But giving in to gut feelings of hatred or revenge is not the God-like approach. Such avenging is in no way a godly thing to do.

Individuals are never right in seeking revenge. The Bible could not be clearer on that. Consider Romans, Chapter 12: "Beloved, do not avenge yourselves, but rather give place to wrath; for it is written, 'vengeance is mine, I will repay; says the Lord.' Therefore 'if your enemy is hungry, feed him; If he is thirsty, give him a drink; for in so doing you will heap coals of fire on his head.' Do not be overcome by evil, but overcome evil with good" (vv. 19-21).

When Jesus hung on the cross, he sought no revenge. Instead, he prayed, "Father, forgive them for they know not what they do." The spirit of Jesus is what we should seek in our own lives when dealing with evildoers. It's not that we sanction evil; it's just that God has shown us a better way through Christ for dealing with it.

Clarence Jordan, my spiritual mentor, said that God's people should be like a lightening rod, taking evil and grounding it instead of hurling it back in a fit of revenge. He further said that if we practice the old revenge concept of "an eye for an eye," then eventually everybody will be blind.

Martin Luther King, Jr. talked about redemptive suffering. He taught that accepting hurts and not responding was a better approach than lashing back at the oppressors. King, of course, got much of his thinking from Jesus and from Gandhi, the Indian nationalist leader who advocated peace and nonviolence.

I know it is difficult to apply such a hard teaching, especially when there has been a real hurt, perhaps a theft, a betrayal, a grave injury, or even a death. But it's in the tough situations of life that we must live out

God's ideas of love, forgiveness, and reconciliation. The old ways certainly haven't brought peace to this world. Maybe we ought to consider accepting hurts and not responding with violence. Maybe we should try to overcome evil with good.

Are you willing to give it a try? There will be casualties, of course, because not everybody reciprocates with kindness and love. But the "eye for an eye" approach has casualties, too. And, I submit, there will be fewer hurts and deaths following God's way than there will be going down the path of retaliation and revenge.

I believe a lot more creativity is needed in dealing with evil deeds, whether those evil deeds are committed against an individual or against a nation. Peace is the desired outcome. What response will sow seeds of peace rather than planting seeds for future hatred, hurt, and warfare?

One of the most difficult things to do in life is to see and understand a situation from another person's point of view. Why did that person or group of people lash out at us? Seeking to understand where the other side "is coming from" is a crucial first step in formulating a creative response that is different from just branding those other people as "evil" and devoid of any redeeming features. The attitude that "God is on our side" and that the other side is completely "of the devil" will justify any reaction we decide to make.

On the other hand, if we stand humbly before God, acknowledging that we are sinners, subject to evil thoughts and evil deeds just as others are, we are more likely to find God's way of peace rather than perpetuating hatred and violence.

Some would say that "Give peace a chance" is a cliché from a by-gone era, but I believe it is a good phrase and should be prayerfully considered as we struggle to be part of making the world a better place for everybody.

One thing is for certain. We must think and pray about this matter-*before* hurt and violence occur because, if we do not, the response is certain—hit back and get revenge. That is the visceral, animal instinct in all of us. If something different and better is desired, it has to be the result of a thoughtful and prayerful process, with God squarely in the middle of it.

So I would say, "Think peace." Think about resolving the problem, long-term, rather than simply hitting back and getting even. There really is, I am convinced, a better way than the way of revenge.

SHORT LINES

I give a lot of commencement speeches at colleges and universities. I always feel privileged and glad to have that opportunity to share my thoughts, ideas, and challenges with graduates who are about to embark on a lifetime of applying what they've learned during their years of study.

I remember one particular commencement address I gave at Ottawa University in Ottawa, Kansas. In that speech I challenged the students to seek out the short lines in life and get in one of those lines to serve. I pointed out that there are both long and short lines in the job market. The long lines are where the very desirable jobs are found. Good working conditions, great pay, bright associates, and interesting challenges. The short lines are for less appealing jobs, with not such good pay, less desirable working conditions, and so forth. Not so many people apply for such jobs, even though the need may be great. Many times, I said, unless you apply, there will be no applicants. I encouraged the students to get into some of the short lines of life.

Jesus taught that we should seek a life of service. If you want to be first, he said, you should be last. Be a servant. Don't seek to elevate yourself. Rather, strive to be a servant and lift up others. To me, what Jesus was teaching was, in reality, the philosophy of the short line.

Years ago, Linda and I made a trip to Papua New Guinea in the South Pacific to plant the seed for Habitat for Humanity. While there, we met a remarkable man in Port Moresby, the capital of that country. His name was James Ferguson. He was a medical doctor from Australia and he'd had a lifetime of missionary service in China and Papua New Guinea. When we met him he was in his early retirement years, but still going strong, working primarily with "rascals," who were members of urban youth gangs in the slum areas of Port Moresby. Dr. Ferguson became one of the principal people who brought Habitat to that country. Many hundreds of houses have been built there in several locations and the work continues to expand steadily.

One day, Dr. Ferguson told us how he became a missionary. He said he was a teenage lad in his native Australia and an old missionary to China came to his church. The old man talked to the youth of the church and challenged them to be missionaries in China. He told the young people there were three reasons why they should go to China as missionaries—dirt, danger, and disease.

Dr. Ferguson said the missionary expounded at some length on each of the three reasons. He said China, in those days and in the areas where missionaries would work, was very dirty. He said everything was dirty and it was difficult to keep anything clean. He went on to say that the country was dangerous. The political situation was unstable and one's very life was at stake in the country as a missionary. Finally, he pointed out that disease was rampant and that staying healthy was difficult.

Dr. Ferguson said that the missionary didn't talk at all about friendly people, nice sunsets, beautiful landscapes, or anything like that—only dirt, danger, and disease. But, Dr. Ferguson said, the message was so compelling that he went forward that night to commit himself to a life of missionary service and so did several other young people.

When we met him, Dr. Ferguson had already served for more than thirty years in China and Papua New Guinea as a missionary. Dr. Ferguson definitely got in a short line with few job applicants, but his life had made a difference and, I might add, he was one of the most radiant and joyous men I've ever had the privilege of knowing.

Often, I believe, young people are seduced by the glamour of big salaries and attractive retirement plans, and they don't even consider the option of a short-line job. As a consequence, their lives are not as rich and full as they could be, and urgent needs in the world are not met.

So I would say to young people, especially, but to people of all ages, consider the short lines of life. As you do, ponder the words of Jesus, "He who finds his life will lose it, and he who loses his life for my sake will find it" (Matthew 10:39).

Look for a short line. It may just lead you to awesome joy, fulfillment, and a meaningful life of service.

AVOID GETTING STUCK IN A RUT

All of us are creatures of habit. We wake up in the morning, brush our teeth, comb our hair, dress, eat breakfast, and drive to work. Routines differ, of course, for different people. But we all have routines. Day after day and week after week we do pretty much the same things, over and over.

Routines are not all bad. And good habits are desirable. Systematically brushing teeth, drinking orange juice, servicing the car, exercising every day, going to worship regularly—all of that and more— are good. But a life that is totally lived by routine is boring. Such a life leads to a dulling of the mind and senses.

My spiritual mentor, Clarence Jordan, said that one can get in a rut in life that ultimately leads to a grave. It happens like this. First a person walks in the same place for a long time and a path is cut. Then, over a longer period of time, walking always in the same place, the path deepens until it becomes a rut. Finally, walking in the rut for a long time deepens until there is no way out because the rut is too deep and one discovers that the rut has become a grave. You see, the only difference between a path, a rut, and a grave is depth. Getting off "the beaten path" avoids the "grave" experience. That's a good thing!

Varying one's routine can be very enlightening. I remember taking a mayor of our town on a tour several years ago. I took him down some streets he'd never been on before. He was amazed at what I showed him. "Millard," he exclaimed, "I've lived in Americus all my life, but today you've shown me things I didn't know were here." I got him off his usual routes and took him to places he had never seen before. He was surprised and shocked at some of the poor living conditions he saw.

People not only walk on the same paths in life. They tend to live in certain circles. There is the Presbyterian circle, the Democratic or Republican circle, the liberal circle, the Rotary or Kiwanis circle, the white folks circle, the Catholic circle, or the wealthy circle. Some circles overlap, but we all have our circles, and we usually stay in them. That's where we know what to expect. It's where we are comfortable. But moving into someone else's circle is interesting and a broadening experience in life.

Habitat for Humanity enables people to cross the lines that divide and separate people. In the process, the lives of everyone are enriched. On a building site or in a committee meeting, one is likely to find a Catholic beside a Protestant, a senior citizen working with a high school student, a Jew discussing a problem with a Lutheran, or a liberal woman putting up siding with a conservative man. We call all of that mixing and crossing of circles a part of the "theology of the hammer."

Nature teaches that cross-pollination strengthens any species. The same is true in human relations. Getting out of a rut puts one up in the light because the walls of the rut are no longer blocking the light. Contact with new people and new experiences brings fresh insights and understanding and a lot of excitement.

Someone once said that we tend to be "down" on what we are not "up" on. Getting out of a rut and crossing circle lines brings us into new relationships and exciting new and different experiences that enable us to be "up" on them.

So the message is clear. Stay in old patterns and dig yourself deeper and deeper into the ruts of life, which separate you from both real life and light. Or vary your routine and avoid disintegrating into a deadly grave. And get over into someone else's circle from time to time to experience new things and to broaden your horizons and understanding.

Are you in a rut? What are the circles in which you live? What action could you take to get out of your ruts and cross over into some new and exciting circles that could enrich your life?

Consider these ideas for getting out of a rut and experiencing life in another circle:

- Visit a place of worship next Sunday that is very different from your own.
- Read a magazine, see a movie, or visit a museum that you normally wouldn't choose.
- Go on a trip to a place where people and the culture are different from you and your culture.
- Volunteer for Habitat for Humanity and meet new people and learn new skills.
- Make a list of some things you've always wanted to do but never had the courage to try, and then pick one.

Climb out of your rut by trying new things and moving into circles that will enrich your life.

DON'T GET BOGGED DOWN

One of the greatest impediments to progress in life is getting bogged down or stuck on a problem, task, or issue. As the CEO of an organization with work in more than eighty nations, a staff of hundreds of people, thousands of volunteers, hundreds of thousands of donors, and a steady flow of problems and opportunities, I do not have the luxury of getting bogged down. I must constantly prioritize, decline certain requests, deflect tasks to others, and expedite assignments to be done by assistants or other staff or volunteers within the organization.

In my work as president of Habitat for Humanity International, I travel a lot. Often, I am out of the office for several days at a time. When I return, there is a stack of correspondence and other papers on my desk. It is imperative that I get through everything before going on the next trip which, quite frequently, is within a few days. Thus, I must go as quickly as possible through the stack and deal with everything there.

The top dozen items may be letters that can be answered quite easily. I dictate answers rapidly, moving right on down through the stack. Then I come to a 300-page manuscript that someone has sent for me to read for the purpose of writing an endorsement or a foreword. If I take care of that item, I'm stuck for hours. I get bogged down. So I put it aside and keep moving through the stack. Other matters come up from time to time where a situation or a person demands an inordinate amount of time. If one is not careful, dealing with such can get you totally consumed to the exclusion of other tasks that need attention.

Remaining free of encumbrances makes it possible for me to keep the big picture of the ministry of Habitat focused in my mind. This enables me to take advantage of opportunities and move us steadily ahead in our plan to spread the work to all nations on earth and to promote the idea that all families should have at least a simple, decent place to live.

Whether you are the head of an organization or fill a role that is vastly different from that sort of responsibility, the basic principle is the same: Know what you want and need to accomplish in your role or work, set your sights clearly on the end result you desire, and work steadily and faithfully to achieve it without getting bogged down.

Obviously, unexpected things come along in life and it is unrealistic to think that you'll never be distracted or get bogged down. Consider the 300-page manuscript mentioned earlier, for instance. When I have worked through the stack on my desk, I can go back and spend a bit of time reflecting about that particular request. I make a determination about whether the request is something I think I should do. I assess the amount of time that will be required, then I decide if I can afford that amount of time and if it is worth the time and effort that must be expended.

Other things come up, too, such as family emergencies and matters involving friends and associates that can consume big chunks of time. And of course, there is the need for breaks, entertainment, relaxation, and so forth. But if you want to make your life count and you want to make a difference in the world, there is no substitute for constantly moving ahead to meet your goals.

You've heard the expression, "The road to hell is paved with good intentions." Well, the road to accomplishing your goals in life is full of bogs, and if you don't learn how to avoid them, you and your goals will "go to hell" or some equivalent. You definitely will not realize what you want to accomplish.

What is bogging you down? What can you do to avoid those bogs? Decide what you need to do to better prioritize and organize your life in order to keep from getting bogged down.

PLOWING NEW GROUND

When I was six years old, my father bought a 400-acre farm out in the country, some eight miles from the small cotton-mill town of Lanett, Alabama, where we lived. Some of the land was open and had been farmed in recent years. Most of the land, though, was covered with trees. My dad decided to increase the acreage to be farmed, so that meant clearing some of the trees away and preparing the ground for farming. This process took several years, and I was involved in various ways.

Perhaps the most memorable way was plowing the new ground. In those days, even though some farmers had tractors, my father decided to go the low-budget way, which was with mules. After the tree stumps were removed, we were ready to plow the ground for the first time. A mule would be hitched to a plow and off we would go with the sharp-pointed plow digging into the earth and turning it upside down.

Plowing new ground was an adventure with elements of danger. You see, one never knew what was out there in front of you. The ground had not been touched by a plow for decades, if ever. As I struggled to keep up behind the quick-stepping mule and maintain the handles upright so that the plow could turn the dirt as it should, I quickly learned about two fierce obstacles that were hidden under the surface. One was rocks—some could be classified as boulders. When a large rock was struck it could tumble back over your feet with resulting pain or injury. The boulders would simply bring you to a jarring halt, with the unhappy result of you being impaled on the plow handles.

Another obstacle was roots. The trees had been cut and the stumps removed, but the roots were still there. When the plow would hit a really big one, again, you would come to a jarring halt and be impaled on the handles. If the roots were smaller, the plow would sever them with the result that one or both ends of the severed root would whack you on the shin with great force, causing pain or injury.

So plowing new ground was, in some ways, like going into battle. But, even though there were pain and injuries, the reward was great because new ground is rich in nutrients and crops do well in soil that has not been farmed. "Plowing new ground" in life is like plowing a field in rural Alabama. There is uncertainty and possible pain or injury, but the potential rewards are great.

Have you plowed any new ground lately?

Many people are afraid of "new ground." They prefer to stay in known and safe territory. Nothing is risked by such living. Potential rewards are lost, and the richness of new experiences and new relationships are forfeited. I prefer to seek out new ground. I've done so many times over the course of my lifetime, and I continue to search for "new ground."

When Linda and I left business and struck out on a new path in life, there were numerous uncertainties. Many people thought we were foolish to leave an affluent lifestyle for something so nebulous and uncertain as "seeking to know God's will for our lives." But "plowing that new ground" has led to an incredibly rich and full life.

When we decided to move to Africa with our four children, again, that "new ground" seemed frightening and uncertain. We not only were going to live and work in a very different part of the world, we had to learn a new language, French, which was the official language of Zaire (the former Belgian Congo). Our family moved for three months to Paris, where we learned the language in an immersion course—at least well enough to function in the new country.

Deciding to go into other new and different countries with the work of Habitat for Humanity has always had an element of risk and uncertainty. I specifically remember our decision to take Habitat to Nicaragua at a time when the political situation there was extremely volatile. We were encouraged to go by Don Mosley, a man who has plowed a lot of new ground in his life. He and his wife, Carolyn, were the two primary people who left Koinonia more than twenty years ago to found Jubilee Partners, a Christian community near Comer, Georgia. Jubilee has been committed over the years to taking in refugees from around the world and teaching them English so they can function in the United States or Canada.

Don went down to Nicaragua on behalf of Habitat for Humanity and worked out a plan for us to start building in a remote corner of the country. From that small beginning, the work has expanded to many locations across the country and more than 2,000 houses have been built. Founding regional offices around the world to enhance our ability to better direct the growing work of Habitat was a bold move of plowing new ground, but those offices are now established and doing a great job in Bangkok, Thailand; San José, Costa Rica; Pretoria, South Africa; and Budapest, Hungary.

Is there some "new ground" on your horizon that you should explore in your personal life, in your company, or in a group with which you are associated? What's holding you back? Henry David Thoreau once wrote that most people lead lives of quiet desperation. Does that characterize your life? Would "plowing some new ground" help rid you of some of that desperation?

Don't misunderstand me. There is a difference between faith and foolishness. Stepping out on faith and doing something that is foolhardy are two different things. Risk-taking and utter foolishness are not the same thing. My experience has taught me that taking calculated risks and "plowing new ground" as a faith initiative lead to a much richer and fuller life.

What are you waiting for? Sharpen your plow blade, pick up the handles, and start plowing that new ground. Just watch out for the rocks and roots!

LIFE LESSONS

CONCERN TO THE POINT OF ACTION

In the early years of our marriage, when we would be getting ready to go somewhere, I would ask my wife Linda if she were ready to leave. Very often she would reply, "Yes." I would walk to the door and wait and wait and wait.

"I thought you were ready to go," I would exclaim.

"I am. I'm just putting on my make-up," she'd reply, or "I'm just doing this or that."

After a while I realized that I wasn't asking the right question. "Are you ready?" didn't adequately communicate that I wanted to go *right then*. So I changed the question: "Are you 'walking-out-the-door' ready?" If I got a "Yes" to that question, I knew that we could soon leave.

In a similar way, many people are *concerned* about various things, but not to the point of actually doing something about the matter. I remember an incident in Montgomery, Alabama, when I was in business in that city. An employee of the company was a sensitive and intelligent woman who was concerned about racial discrimination.

One day she came to work very agitated about something that had happened the night before. She told me that she had been in a meeting and some other women there were making all sorts of disparaging comments about African Americans. "I was dismayed by all those racist things being said by those women. I got so upset," she said, "that I almost said something!"

I remember the old gospel hymn that was so popular in revival services when I was growing up in Alabama, "Almost Persuaded." Many people are *almost persuaded* to take action, but something holds them back. Maybe fear, maybe uncertainty, maybe lack of conviction. In any event, there are so many good intentions that never get translated into action. The old cliché rings true: "The road to hell is paved with good intentions."

Good intentions or concern are essential as a starting point to changing things for the better, but concern must be translated into action if actual change is to take place. As the Bible says, we are called to *do* good, not just think good or be concerned about good.

Are there some things in your life that you are concerned about? Should you be taking action to improve or correct those matters?

I suggest that if you are concerned about a situation, think deeply about it. Pray and ask God for guidance and wisdom. Talk the matter over with someone close to you and ask for his or her advice. Then, when you are convinced, based on good information and after making sure that your own heart and motives are pure, take action! Go as far as you can with your personal efforts.

LITTLE THINGS MEAN A LOT

Recently, a dear friend had unexpected surgery. During the time of convalescence, Linda and I sent her a small bouquet of roses. She called when the roses arrived, exclaiming that the roses were precisely the color that was such a favorite of her beloved father. Our friendship, already strong, was strengthened by that simple act of love and concern.

Little things mean a lot. A note to a friend. A letter of encouragement to an acquaintance who is going through a difficult time. A phone call or visit to someone who has experienced a personal loss.

When our family moved from Koinonia Farm to Americus in 1977, we were greeted with coldness and expressions of hostility. Broken glass was thrown in our driveway nearly every night for the first couple of weeks.

I had opened a small law office in town to support our family. One room of that office was the first office of Habitat for Humanity. A local attorney, Frank Myers, Jr., invited Linda and me to dinner at his home. During this visit, he told me that he was aware of the feelings of people toward us because of our connection with Koinonia. He also said he was sure I didn't have a law library since I had not practiced law for several years. He told me I could use his law library "just like it was my own" until

I was able to afford to buy my own law books. I was deeply touched by his simple offer of kindness and support. I used his library for a couple of years and it was a great help to me. The community's negative feelings toward us dissipated over the years, but I'll always remember and appreciate the kindness of Frank Myers. He has remained a friend over the years, expressing that friendship in various ways, including becoming an encourager and supporter of Habitat.

Our house in Americus was located on East Church Street. My law office was about three quarters of a mile away on West Church Street. As I walked to work each morning and back home in the evening, I got into the habit of picking up trash along the way. There was no fanfare to what I did. I simply bent down as I went along and scooped up candy wrappers, coke cans, and other assorted trash that had been tossed on the sidewalk and street by thoughtless people. I put the collected items in trash receptacles. Over time, I began to get comments and even phone calls from people who had noticed what I was doing. They expressed appreciation and, I believe, were inspired to "do likewise."

Also, my daily encounters with trash gave me an insight I had not had before: There is a direct connection between trash on the streets and substandard housing. A community that tolerates trash on the streets will accept substandard housing. Conversely, a community that will not accept trash will not tolerate poverty housing. You see, trash is a visible sign of the mentality of people in an area. That mentality is that the physical environment is of little concern to them. Substandard housing is simply a larger visible sign of a lack of concern.

I have often said that housing is a spiritual issue. Housing is so essential to human beings. Adequate housing promotes all sorts of positive things, especially for children. Lack of good housing creates negative conditions, which precipitate all sorts of bad results in individuals, families, and communities.

Like housing, trash is also a spiritual issue. The earth is the Lord's, the Bible says. Showing respect for the earth demonstrates respect and love for God. In like manner, people are God's creation. Showing respect and love for people demonstrates respect and love for God.

But it all starts out with little stuff. A piece of trash is carelessly tossed on the sidewalk. Pick it up! That just might launch an effort to end poverty housing in your community. A friend needs encouragement? Pick up the phone.

Do little things to show love and respect for those around you, and you will reap big rewards.

STRUGGLE FOR LIFE

I love to pull weeds. I suppose that urge comes from the same place within me that compels me to pick up trash. I don't like to see things in places where they don't belong.

One day I pulled a bunch of weeds from the flower beds in front of our house. I put them on the sidewalk so they would wither and die. That night there was a big shower of rain. The next day, I went outside to check on the weeds and, to my great surprise, the stems were inclining upward, with outstretched leaves seeking maximum exposure to the sun. The roots, although totally exposed and devoid of dirt, were inclining downward, seeking anchor and a foundation for the continuation of life.

As I pondered that remarkable struggle for life, I realized that all of creation is like that. Living things, from lowly weeds to the animals of the earth to human beings, seek to stay alive.

I believe life is God-given. The Bible teaches that God, the Creator, gave life to everything on earth. His final act of creation was mankind. Genesis records the event, "And the Lord God formed man from the dust of the ground, and breathed into his nostrils the breath of life; and man became a living being" (2:7).

While the essential ingredients to sustain life for a plant are simple—soil, moisture, and sunlight—life for human beings is much more complex. Physical things are needed to be sure, such as food, clothing, and shelter. But as the Bible states, "Man does not live by bread alone" (Matthew 4:4).

And humans have a choice. A plant cannot pull itself up out of the ground. Only external forces can kill a plant, but a person can make choices that literally determine life or death.

There is a wonderful monologue from God about this matter that is recorded in Deuteronomy. God's speech was given to the Israelites as they were about to enter the Promised Land at the end of their long pilgrimage from Egypt. Listen to what God said:

> See, I have set before you today life and good, death and evil, in that I command you today to love the Lord your God, to walk in His ways, and to keep His commandments, His statutes, and His judgments, that you may live and multiply; and the Lord your God will bless you in the land which you go to possess. But if your heart turns away so that you do not hear, and are drawn away, and worship other gods and serve them, I announce to you today that you shall surely perish, you shall not prolong your days in the land which you cross over the Jordan to go in and possess. I call heaven and earth as witnesses today against you, that I have set before you life and death, blessing and curse; therefore choose life, that both you and your descendants may live; that you may love the Lord your God, that you may obey His voice, and that you may cling to Him, for He is your life and the length of your days; and that you may dwell in the land which the Lord swore to your fathers, to Abraham, Isaac, and Jacob, to give them. (30:15-20)

So what does all this teach us? It seems clear to me that life is precious because it is God-ordained and God-created. The great humanitarian Albert Schweitzer developed his personal philosophy called "Reverence for Life." He honored and respected all forms of life, and especially human life. He gave his own life seeking to serve the simple and humble village people in his corner of Africa.

Too many people, I think, are flippant about life. There is a certain attitude that some lives are expendable. Especially, for example, if a person crosses a certain threshold in wrongdoing, he should forfeit his own life.

For several years, after returning to Georgia from our time of missionary service in Africa, I practiced law. A part of my practice was defending murder cases. In several of those cases, the state was seeking the death penalty. In impaneling a jury, I had the right to question prospective jurors. I was intrigued to discover in that questioning, called *voir dire*, that almost all African Americans in south Georgia oppose the death penalty and almost all whites are in favor of it. Typically, when I would ask the question to a black person about the death penalty, he or she would reply, "Two wrongs don't make a right." I was fascinated by that simple philosophy.

Why do whites, almost all of whom are Christian, support the death penalty, while black Christians, living in the same area and reading the same Bible, oppose it? I think the answer lies in the different life experiences of the two groups. Whites historically have been the dominant group, making laws and enforcing them. Blacks, on the other hand, have received the harsh consequences of the law. They are the ones who have been jailed and killed in disproportionate numbers by the white man's law. In the process, they have become more forgiving and more grateful for life. They are not as willing to execute harsh judgment on the wrongdoers as are the whites.

But God is no respecter of persons. God is not white or black. God is Spirit and one must deal with God in spirit and in truth. Truth reveals that God is on the side of life. God gives life and God blesses life. Those who desire life and life full of abundance and meaning must obey God and, in the admonition of Scripture, "Cling to God, for He is your life and the length of your days" (Deuteronomy 30:20).

At Habitat for Humanity, we cherish life. Families forced to live in poor conditions are chosen to work with Habitat volunteers to build or renovate simple but good and solid houses. Life is enriched and not only in a physical sense. The recipient families experience God's love through the generous, caring volunteers with whom they work to build the house, and everyone is blessed and drawn closer to God.

Linda and I have been privileged to participate in countless dozens of Habitat house dedication services over the years. Songs of praise are sung.

Words of thanks and joy are spoken about the sponsor and volunteers who made the build possible. Prayers are lifted up to God. And keys and a Bible are presented to the new homeowners. Then, almost without exception, there is a great outpouring of emotion by the homeowner family, usually expressed by shouts of joy and uncontrollable sobbing. Above all, the homeowners give praise and honor to God. In everything, life is affirmed and celebrated.

In the ancient Holy Land, God put a choice before the people: "life and good or death and evil." The choice is still before us. Choose life and good, for God's sake and for your own.

RANDOM HAPPENINGS

I was sitting by a sliding glass door at Glencove in north Georgia working on this book. My back was to the door and all was quiet and calm—a perfect setting for writing. All of sudden, there was a loud thump. I jumped up and looked behind me to see two birds lying on the ground. One was fluttering slightly and the other one was sitting up, facing away from me, rocking back and forth, obviously dizzy and disoriented.

My wife, Linda, in the adjoining room, yelled out, "Did you see that? Those two birds came soaring down, one apparently chasing the other and they just went, headlong, into the glass door. I happened to be looking out the window and I saw them crash into the glass."

I looked back at the birds. They were beautiful brown thrashers. The one lying flat was now perfectly still. Apparently, his neck was broken. Death had come instantly. The other one still rocked gently back and forth. I stood there and gazed at them for a long while, pondering the sudden and violent event. Then I went back to my writing. Some minutes later, I looked back at the place where the birds had fallen. The dead one, of course, was there, but the other one was gone. Obviously, he was only stunned by the crash, so he recovered and returned to the forest.

I reflected on that little episode. A random happening. Two birds in the woods. Playing or fighting, I don't know which, but the excitement of the moment made them less than fully aware of their surroundings so they crashed into a glass window. One died instantly; the other recovered and flew away.

Life is like that, isn't it? For birds, other animals, and for human beings. Things go along quietly and nicely and then—*boom!*—something dramatic, sudden, and violent happens. And, for reasons difficult to explain, one person is killed or maimed for life and another walks away.

How can one explain such events? I don't think you can. Stuff happens. Good stuff, bad stuff, and everything in between.

The Bible says it "rains" on the just and the unjust (Matthew 5:45). I do believe in the power of prayer, but I do not believe that prayer and its power make anyone immune from "rain" and other external forces. If a bird or a person crashes into an immovable object there will be negative consequences—either death or a gigantic headache or worse!

In embracing and seeking to live a godly life, one is not exempted from the forces of gravity or other natural forces in the world. If a person, godly or not, jumps from a high building, the force of gravity will take the body down and, depending on the height, will do varying amounts of damage when there is the sudden slam into the water or the ground.

Jesus dealt with this issue at the beginning of his ministry when the devil led him into the wilderness and tempted him in various ways, including encouraging him to leap from a high place so the angels could rescue him. He rejected the temptation and, in effect, said one should accept the forces of nature and work in harmony with them and not call on God to do miracles or make magic to save you.

As one journeys through life, things do happen, to one personally and to others. Some things come into our lives slowly, but others come crashing in with a shock and suddenness that takes one's breath and sometimes health or life away.

Not long ago, I was talking on the phone with a dear friend. He and I had been friends for many years. He was an extremely intelligent, faith-filled, and generous man. We were laughing and talking for several minutes. His wife, also a good friend, got on the phone and I enjoyed a good time of conversation with her.

A few weeks later, I got a terse note from a mutual friend of the man on the phone, "Millard, you should know that Bob has dementia. The prognosis is not good."

Dementia? How could that be? Just days ago he was so normal, talking, joking, and laughing, completely in his right mind.

My own dear mother, at age twenty-seven, got sick in the afternoon and was dead by midnight. I was an only child and three years old. My father was devastated.

Natural disasters and human-made tragedies like that of September 11, 2001, leave people reeling. Some people die or are grievously injured. Others live through such events unscathed.

At Habitat for Humanity, we have had an amazingly good record of our houses surviving natural disasters, both in the United States and in other countries. When Hurricane Andrew hit south Florida in 1992, for example, we didn't lose a single house, while thousands of other houses around the Habitat houses blew away. In Central America, when Hurricane Mitch roared through in November of 1998, we lost very few houses.

How does one explain that? First of all, we just lift up hands and hearts in praise and thanksgiving to God. We don't understand everything. But I do know that our people are conscientious in trying to locate Habitat houses in good places, away from flood plains or other disaster-prone areas. When we must build in such places, we make sure hurricane protection is built into the houses, including clamps and iron strips to hold the trusses tightly in place. And we make sure that adequate nails are in place to secure the roof and the siding on the houses in the event of a natural disaster.

How does one deal with sudden and random happenings? It has been said that the success of a person in life is not dependent on what happens to him or her, but on how a person *responds* to what happens.

I believe that a vibrant faith can and does sustain a person in times of crisis. I have known of people who became angry with God because of certain catastrophic events in life. That, to me, is futile. God isn't punishing a person by such events. They just happen. But God is present to support and sustain us, no matter what. That force in the universe is above all others. However, it does not cancel out the others, nor does it exempt anyone from the uncertainties of life.

Again, God does not exempt us from the natural forces in the world. We must accept those forces and work in harmony with them. Then, when something unexpected and negative happens for whatever reason, we must simply pick up the pieces, thank and praise God for what's left, and move forward in life.

STAYING HEALTHY

Good health is a blessing. It is also a responsibility. The Bible teaches that the body is the dwelling place of the Holy Spirit. If that is true, then each person has the obligation to keep that dwelling place clean, wholesome, strong, and healthy.

The person who has been the greatest inspiration to me about health is former President Jimmy Carter. At every stage in his life, he has been diligent in taking care of himself and keeping his body and mind strong and healthy. As a consequence, even in his late 70s, he is able to work a full day of hard labor, sometimes to the chagrin of younger workers, and he is able to travel the world and be engaged in a wide array of activities, many of which require strong vigor and robust health.

Many people, unfortunately, do not take care of themselves. They abuse alcohol, smoke cigarettes, eat foods that are injurious to the body, do not get proper rest, neglect routine health measures such as exercise and good hygiene, and then they seem surprised when their health fails. You've heard the saying, "the chickens come home to roost." There are consequences to our actions.

Of course, some things happen that are beyond our control. A birth defect. An unfortunate car wreck. A freak fall. Even with such impediments, though, one should, as the bantam hen, do what you can with what you've got. It is fruitless and pointless to weep over what you don't have. Rather, one should thank God for what one does have and preserve it to the best of one's ability.

I have always tried to keep myself in good health. As a youth, I participated in every sport that was available—football, baseball, basketball, and track. I well remember the suffering I experienced at practice and in games when my body cried out to stop. But I pushed on, determined to stay in the game. I was moderately talented, but I believed that the competition was good and healthy for me. Those activities gave me an appreciation for "being in shape." That was, and is, a great feeling.

I remember so vividly the training Linda and I did in the early 1980s to do our first marathon walk for Habitat for Humanity from Americus, Georgia, to Indianapolis, Indiana. We honed our bodies and, when the day came for us to launch the walk, we were ready. As we consistently walked fifteen to twenty miles a day for forty straight days, it felt great to have strong legs and healthy bodies to serve us well along the way. The purpose of the walk, incidentally, was to raise awareness of and funds for Habitat for Humanity. The destination of the walk, Indianapolis, was the site of our seventh Anniversary Celebration.

I have discovered that walking is one of the best forms of exercise. Linda and I walk a lot. In addition to the long walk to Indianapolis, we also organized and participated in marathon walks from Americus to Kansas City (1,000 miles); Portland, Maine, to Atlanta (1,200 miles—we walked a little less than half of that one); and Americus to Atlanta (140 miles). These walks were also in connection with milestone anniversaries of Habitat for Humanity—the tenth in 1986, the twelfth in 1988, and the twentieth in 1996.

Both of us walk every week. Often and for days at a time, we walk every day. Usually, we walk a mile to three or four miles at a time. Such exercise keeps legs strong and the whole body toned up.

I also exercise in the usual course of my activities. When traveling—and that's a lot—I try to walk in airline terminals rather than take a train or get on the moving sidewalks. Likewise, when in a hotel, I prefer to walk up and down the stairs rather than use the elevator. When flying, especially on long flights, I try to get up and stretch often and walk up and down the aisles.

Sometimes when I wake up at night, I take a few minutes to do exercises. Such stretching and flexing the muscles feels good. The exercise also gets the heart pumping and tires the body. Hence, when I lie back down in the bed, I fall right back to sleep. Simple habits like these keep one stronger and healthier.

I have never smoked and I have never consumed alcohol in anything but moderate amounts. I credit my father for keeping me from those vices. My dad didn't drink alcohol at all, but he smoked incessantly. Indeed, he died at a relatively young age from smoking. As I was growing up, he told me repeatedly that he had gotten himself addicted to cigarettes and he didn't have the willpower to quit. He pleaded with me, successfully, not ever to get myself addicted to tobacco. I loved my father and greatly admired and respected him. As I said above, I never went against his counsel on tobacco or alcohol.

Some people seem to have good health as a gift from God. But good health practices will make even the healthiest and most blessed person feel stronger and be better equipped to go about life's activities. Also, routine physical examinations should be a regular part of your life to discover any emerging health problems that can be treated and, hopefully, cured as soon as possible.

Yes, good health is a blessing, but it is also a responsibility. Are you being responsible about your health? How could you improve your physical well-being?

Take action to maintain a strong and healthy body and mind.

AGING GRACEFULLY

Our oldest daughter, Kim, lives with her husband, Jim Isakson, and their two boys, Zachary and Alexander, in Colleyville, Texas. Linda and I visit them several times a year as we travel in connection with our work with Habitat for Humanity.

On one such visit, I was down on the floor playing with the eldest son, Zachary. At the time, he was about four years old. He looked up at me and inquired, "Granddaddy, are you an old man?"

"What do you think, Zachary?"

He thought for a moment and declared, "No, I don't think so." We resumed our play. After a while I did something—I've forgotten exactly what—that irritated him. He exclaimed loudly, "You *are* an old man!"

Several years earlier, I was walking on the sidewalk in front of the tour center of Habitat for Humanity International in Americus. The young daughter of one of our volunteer couples ran out from the center and leaped up into my arms. I scooped her up and faced her back toward some playmates who were standing on the porch. She squealed, "This is my granddaddy!"

I remember distinctly the shock I felt at being called "granddaddy." I had long been a father but at that time I had no grandchildren. I've always loved children, and I seem to quickly develop a good rapport with them. I had been called "daddy" by my own children and by others, but the day that I heard "granddaddy" for the first time was a shock.

I also remember being in Hartford, Connecticut, a few years ago on a speaking trip. An article appeared in the local newspaper and it described me as a "silver-haired" man. That was a shock. I had some gray hairs, but I didn't think of myself as "silver-haired."

A similar experience was at a hotel counter when the clerk told me I was entitled to a senior discount. I remember thinking, "This young woman sees me as an old man." That's not the image I had of myself, but the reality was that she didn't see me the way I saw myself.

Aging is like that. It comes slowly and quietly and, at the same time, sooner than you expect. Some people go into denial about their age. I've seen women in their fifties and sixties dress as if they were in their twenties. And some men do the same thing. It seems to me that embracing and accepting one's age is so much better and healthier than trying to hang on to an age that has passed. That's not to say, of course, that one should not try to stay as healthy and active as possible at every age and stage of life.

The person who best exemplifies aging gracefully, I think, is former President Jimmy Carter. As this book is being written, he is seventy-seven years old. He embraces that age in life in an incredibly positive way. He is still robust and vigorous, with an active travel and work schedule. His mind is sharp and he is constantly engaged in activities that keep him mentally engaged and alert. But he doesn't try to deny or hide his age in any way. He rejoices in being an ex-president. He revels in being a grandfather. He is content with being a senior citizen.

I remember so well sitting beside President Carter in Hungary in 1996 when we were together there for the annual Jimmy Carter blitz build. The two of us were being interviewed by a Dutch TV crew. The interviewer asked President Carter, "Mr. President, you have been a state senator, governor, and president. What was the best time of your life?"

Without hesitation, President Carter replied, "Right now. This is the best time."

I was surprised and delighted by his answer. It reminded me of the strong teaching in the Bible that "today is the day of salvation" (2 Corinthians 6:2). The connotation of that concept is that the current time is what God has given us. Yesterday has gone and tomorrow has not yet come. Today is what we have. It's God's gift to us. It is life. It is ours to squander or to cherish and make the most of. And that's true at every age of life.

Some years ago I recall reading a powerful little book by Thomas Kelly titled A *Testament of Devotion* (San Francisco: HarperSanFrancisco, 1996). In that book, he talked about the concept of "the eternal now." He pointed out that many people dwell on the past, rethinking and seeking to relive that which has passed, or they worry about the future and all of its uncertainties. In the process they miss the present, which is seen as rather inconsequential in that it only connects the past with the future. But, Kelly points out, the present is life. It is the only time we have in which to live and carry out life's activities.

In my work with Habitat for Humanity, it is a great joy to meet so many retirement-age people who are so actively involved in the work. These are the people who make up a great percentage of the tens of thousands of people who sit on local Habitat boards and committees all across the United States and in countries around the world. Literally thousands of these senior citizens are routinely on local work crews building Habitat houses. They have a variety of names for their crews: "The over-the-hill gang," "the Wednesday crew," "Seniors for Habitat," and so forth.

Also, there is the RV Care-a-Vanner program, which involves largely retirement-age couples traveling across the country in caravans to build Habitat houses. Thousands of people are now involved in that exciting effort.

One of the great things about all of these senior citizens being so actively and dynamically involved in the ministry of Habitat is that they are able to work directly with the equally large numbers of young people who are involved. It is proving to be such a blessing to both the young and the old that they can work closely together. There is transference of knowledge, especially from the senior citizens to the youth. And the elders get a full dose of youthful enthusiasm and fresh insights about things, too.

Jesus said, "I came that you might have life and have it abundantly" (John 10:10). That abundant life is possible at all stages of life. So my advice to myself and to you is to grow old gracefully, accepting the advancing years as a gift from God and as a God-given opportunity to be engaged in meaningful and productive activities that enrich our own lives as well as the lives of others.

IMPORTANCE OF STUDY

The Apostle Paul wrote to young Timothy that he should "study to show thyself approved unto God, a workman that needs not to be ashamed, rightly dividing the word of truth" (2 Timothy 2:15). It is certainly important for a young person to study not only the Bible, but other things as well. I believe God expects each person to develop his or her potential to the highest degree possible. Our minds and talents are gifts from God. What we do with those God-given endowments is up to each individual.

I have written that a person should consider the "short lines" of life. That is to say, a dedicated person who wants to make his or her life count and make a difference should prayerfully consider tasks and jobs that few others desire to do. But, whether one gets in the "short lines" or "long lines" of life, the imperative should be the same to develop God-given talents and minds to the greatest extent possible.

The development of our intellects is accomplished by study. Some study is done in a highly organized way in schools of various kinds or in study groups. Other study is accomplished privately. But all study has the same purpose of expanding our knowledge and understanding of the subject matter.

Study is extremely important for young people, but study should also remain a priority throughout life. A person who has long impressed and inspired me in regard to study is Jimmy Carter. Even though he has made many truly incredible marks in his life and is a huge success by any measurement, he remains curious about a large array of subjects and he studies constantly to keep improving himself and expanding his knowledge.

Recently, he was at Habitat headquarters in Americus to make a Habitat promotional video. While there, he had an extensive conversation with Kim MacDonald, our talented staff photographer. He was interested in learning from her because he was planning to photograph items of furniture that he had made over the years and publish a book of those photographs.

Most Sundays, Jimmy Carter teaches Sunday school at little Maranatha Baptist Church in Plains. Since Linda and I are members there (Jimmy Carter recruited us), we often hear him teach. And, without fail, it is abundantly clear that he has studied the lesson and is totally prepared to teach.

Studying, especially studying a subject that is new and different, is not all joy. A certain amount of pain is associated with serious study, but rewards are in abundance. The discipline of study sharpens the mind and makes it easier to learn other subjects.

There is a tendency in some people to "settle in," to know a limited subject fairly well and to be content with that. Such complacency may give temporary comfort, but it doesn't bode well over the long term. Life is change. Indeed, the only "constant" in life is change. If a person does not continually study to stay abreast of change, he or she gets left behind. So study is not just a good idea, it is essential to staying abreast of things and keeping one's mind alert, ready to deal with a changing environment.

At Habitat for Humanity, I realized a few years ago that we needed to formalize study to keep people learning on a regular basis and in a systematic way. I proposed a Habitat for Humanity University to equip people, especially young people, to be a vital part of this movement to end the shame and disgrace of poverty housing and homelessness.

Nic Retsinas, head of the Joint Center for Housing Studies at Harvard University and a very active member of the Habitat for Humanity International board of directors, is heading a task force to create Habitat for Humanity University. The mission statement of the new university will be "To train and inspire leadership to lead the growing worldwide movement to end poverty housing and homelessness."

Already, several initiatives have been launched to promote and enhance study within Habitat for Humanity. In Africa, for example, Harry Goodall, vice president of Habitat's work on the continent of Africa and in the Middle East, has created the Habitat Academy, a study program to regularly train and equip Habitat leaders in more than twenty countries where Habitat is building throughout Africa and the Middle East.

Ted Swisher, vice president of Habitat's work in the United States, has collaborated with Duke University to set up a certification program for executive directors of U.S. Habitat affiliates to enable those directors to study in a systematic way in order to improve their leadership skills.

Other study programs have been inaugurated, including the annual workshops that are held at regional meetings all across the United States. But the most impressive study program of all was the brainchild of Ed Johnson, president of Sterling College in Sterling, Kansas. He conceived of setting up a group of Habitat for Humanity Fellows. These Fellows would study at Sterling for four years on full scholarship. They would study various subjects, including social entrepreneurship. At the end of their college career, the Fellows would work for a minimum of one year for Habitat for Humanity, either at a local Habitat affiliate or for Habitat International at a regional office or at the international headquarters.

The first class of twenty-five Fellows enrolled at Sterling in the fall of 2001. It is anticipated that each fall another class of twenty-five will enter. Furthermore, over time, it is hoped that the program at Sterling will grow and that it will be adopted by other colleges and universities in the United States and abroad. Hoseo University of Asan, Korea, is considering the program as well.

Study is essential in a dynamic program like Habitat for Humanity, and it is likewise necessary in other organizations and for individuals.

"Study to show thyself approved unto God . . . so as not to be ashamed, rightly dividing the word of truth." To be a faithful and diligent student of God's word was Paul's advice to Timothy. That advice is still sound today and is applicable to other subjects. Using and constantly developing and expanding your God-given intellect is something that everyone should strive to do throughout life.

What course of study are you in today that is enhancing and expanding your knowledge? Of what subject or subjects? Do you make a regular practice of studying God's word? If not, why not?

Keep your mind sharp and expand your talents by pursuing a life devoted to learning.

RADICAL COMMON SENSE

Several years ago, I was at a speaking engagement at the University of Akron in Ohio. A student was introducing me and his concluding comment was one I'll never forget. "We're glad to have Mr. Fuller with us today. He heads Habitat for Humanity, an organization that practices radical common sense." I was so impressed with his insight into what Habitat for Humanity is all about.

The work of Habitat is radical in three key ways. First, we have a radical goal, namely, to completely eliminate poverty housing and homelessness. We believe *every* family, every person, should have, as a minimum, a simple, decent place to live.

Second, we use a radical finance plan. No profit and no interest. The idea comes from the Bible. See Exodus 22:25, which states that, when lending to the poor, do not charge interest. That teaching, incidentally, is found in all three of the monotheistic religions, namely Islam, Judaism, and Christianity. Even so, it is considered radical actually to do business with that idea. In general, in the western world, the lowest interest rate is usually reserved for the wealthiest people. It's called the prime-lending rate. The highest interest rate is charged to the poor. Habitat for

Humanity, though, follows the ancient scriptural principle of charging no interest to the poor. We call it "God's finance plan."

The third way in which Habitat for Humanity is radical is that we employ the "theology of the hammer," which teaches that true religion must be more than singing and talking. Action is required, and the theology embraces a wide array of people and organizations. Individuals, churches, and other groups, both religious and political, disagree on many things—abortion, the death penalty, homosexuality, welfare reform, health care, and so forth. Habitat brings everybody together to build and renovate houses. On work sites and at board and committee meetings, you'll find Protestants, Catholics, Jews, Latter-Day Saints, democrats, republicans, rich, poor, black, white, male, female, young, old, and everybody in between. That's radical! I even saw Jimmy Carter and Newt Gingrich carrying a board of sheetrock one day at a build in Kentucky! And women are building houses all around the world. They are doing everything—carpentry, roofing, plumbing, and electrical work. That's radical. The men are preparing the meals and refreshments. That's even more radical!

The radical, however, is balanced by common sense. You see, it is the very essence of common sense that people who get sleepy at night should have a good place in which to sleep on terms they can afford to pay.

It is common sense that children, especially, should have decent housing, so they can grow up to be all that God intended.

It is common sense that people of faith should work together to express God's love in a program that is agreed upon. Christians, in particular, should not disagree on everything. It is common sense that denominations of a wide diversity of opinion about a host of things should work together to demonstrate God's love by building and renovating houses for families in need.

It is common sense that people should be helped in a way that does not foster dependency. That's why Habitat for Humanity does not give away houses. That's why we employ "sweat equity," whereby the prospective homeowners must put in hundreds of hours of labor building their own home and houses for others. Then, when the house is finished, the family moves in and repays the no-interest mortgage over a period of years. All of that is common sense.

And, it seems to me that it is just pure common sense that organizations such as Habitat for Humanity are needed to promote reconciliation in a fragmented and often violent world.

Furthermore, this whole concept of radical common sense has application beyond Habitat for Humanity. In the life of an individual, for instance, it's not good or advisable to be so radical in ideas or actions that one lacks common sense and loses all respect of associates. On the other hand, a totally safe and secure life with no risk or adventures is utterly boring.

As a Christian, my model is Jesus. He surely was a radical in so many ways, but he was not a wild-eyed person with no contact with neighbors and associates. Apparently, he was quite conventional in dress and general demeanor. He abided by most customs of his day. His radicalness was brought about by his total devotion to God. He was absolutely committed to his heavenly Father. That commitment was paramount, and if it brought him into conflict with society, so be it. Such a commitment to God was, and is, considered radical. If one reflects deeply, the conclusion must be that complete devotion to God is also the ultimate in common sense.

The great reformer, Martin Luther, once wrote, "let goods and kindred go, this mortal life also . . . ." That's a radical statement motivated by Jesus, but it is also the very essence of common sense.

One of the simplest and yet most profound questions in the Bible is this, "What does it profit a man to gain the whole world and lose his own soul?" (Mark 8:36). Scripture is laced with the contrast between the radical and common sense. "If you want to find yourself, you must lose yourself. . . .He who would be first must be servant of all. . . .You must become as a little child. . . .You must be born again."

When I left a very successful business career to do the humble work of helping the poor, many people thought I was crazy. I well remember a couple coming to see Linda and me at the small Koinonia community near Americus, Georgia. After visiting for a while, the man exclaimed, "You look so normal!" I asked him what he meant by that comment. "Well," he continued, "the word back in Montgomery is that you had a mental breakdown and had come over here to Georgia to get well."

You see, leaving a successful career, giving away our money, and working in a program to help very poor people was considered so radical that I must be having mental problems. But the truth was that I was dealing with a larger issue of my physical and spiritual health and that of my family. I wanted to put my life more in line with what I believed God wanted me to be doing, and when one takes the long look at life, what shows more common sense than desiring to live in accordance with God's will? So the radical and common sense, as opposite as they seem, can come together beautifully in the life of an individual as well as in an organization to produce a positive result.

What is radical in your life? Are you being radical in a positive way or a destructive way? Is your radicalness in line with God's will for your life, or are you simply rebellious? Where is the common sense in your life or in your church or organization? Is that common sense simply boring, or is it positive common sense that is enriching your life, your church, and your community?

Practice radical common sense to achieve great things.

GIFTS

GOD AT THE END OF THE ROPE

My experience has taught me that once a person has sensed God's general call in life and is "off and running" in fulfilling that call, God honors and is intimately involved in any ensuing activity. But God wants to be a co-creator, a co-partner in our endeavors. He has no interest in doing it all.

Very often, I have seen people of faith make a serious mistake in simply sitting back and waiting for God to take care of things. That's not the way it works. God expects us to use our God-given brains and our God-given talents to do all we know how to do to move ahead with the activity at hand. If we do that, God will be there with us and, quite often, rather amazing things happen.

Let me tell you an exciting story that illustrates what I'm talking about. I call it the "God at the end of the human rope" factor.

When I was in Africa with my family serving as a missionary and building houses for needy families, we ran out of construction iron rods to go in the cement lentils, which are installed above the doors and windows of each house. We couldn't find those iron rods anywhere. Blocks had been laid for a number of houses up to the top of the window and door openings, but we couldn't go any higher with the blocks without the lentils and we couldn't pour any lentils without the iron rods. We were stuck. I was determined to move ahead, though, so I continued to search everywhere for the essential iron rods.

We were living and working in Mbandaka, the capital city of Equator Region in Zaire (the former Belgian Congo). The city was situated right on the banks of the Congo River. Several years earlier in colonial days, the Belgians had put in a cement wall along the edge of the river. That wall was to be part of a port. Unfortunately, the wall was poorly engineered so it started to crack and slowly drift out into the river. The port project was abandoned but the old cracking wall was still there.

As I examined the wall one day, I observed that iron rods, exactly like we needed for the lentils, were exposed in the large cracks in the concrete. The exposed pieces were not too long and there were a limited number of them. It would be treacherous to hang out over the river and try to salvage them. But I had no other source for the iron rods.

I found a hacksaw and, with a couple of helpers, started to salvage the needed rods. As this work was proceeding and after a dozen or so rods had been salvaged, I noticed a truck race past us on a dirt road that ran parallel to the river some twenty or thirty yards away.

As the truck roared past, a dust cloud billowed behind it. Then, all of a sudden, the truck slammed on the brakes and stopped. It backed up and turned down the path leading to where we were hanging out over the river, cutting the iron rods.

"What are you doing?" the driver yelled.

"Salvaging some iron rods from this old port."

"Why?"

I climbed down and explained our work with the church in building houses for needy families. The man had heard of our work but had not seen the houses. He explained that he worked with the Wimpy Construction Company out of Great Britain and that the company was in town to extend the runway on the local airport.

"Your project sounds like a good one," he said, "How many of the iron rods do you need?"

I told him we were building 114 houses and that we only had enough rods for about 14 houses. So, I said, we need rods for a hundred houses.

"Well," he replied, "we can donate the rods to you. Get down off that old wall before you kill yourself and go back to building houses!"

A few days later, a big Wimpy truck drove up and dumped brand new iron rods for a hundred houses. The company ended up helping us in other ways for many months to come.

To me this is an excellent example of doing all you know how to do and in doing that, something wonderful and unexpected happens. If I had simply gone into my room to pray for the iron rods, I wouldn't have gotten any. But because we prayed and then took action, doing all we knew how to do, the "God equation" kicked in.

I've seen this dynamic happen time and time again, especially in my work with Habitat for Humanity. What we do in building houses with and for families in need is God's work. Being involved in it is God's claim on my life and on the lives of countless thousands of others. When we ask for God's help and then go to work to do all that can be done, God is there, usually right at the end of our human rope or, sometimes, at the end of an iron rod.

Have you experienced this dynamic in your life? Or, perhaps you currently have a matter of great concern that you are praying about. Should you be doing something in addition to simply praying?

The old adage is true—"God helps those who help themselves." If you take the first step, God will bless your efforts abundantly.

LOVE

David Castle is a retired college professor. He and wife Ellie have lived and worked at Koinonia Farm near Americus, Georgia, for several years. David is one of the kindest and gentlest men I have ever met. He is also a deep thinker and a peacemaker. He says that he tries to live by the integrity of love more than by purity of belief. That, he reasons, puts relationships ahead of doctrine.

The core teaching of Jesus is to love. He said that everybody should be loved, even enemies. He posed the powerful question one day, "If you love only those who love you, what reward do you have? Even sinners do that" (Matthew 5:46).

I well remember Habitat staffer David Snell leading a work team of evangelical Protestants to Mexico to build Habitat houses. David recalls the conversation on the way down. The work team members were eager to "share Christ" with the Mexicans who, they assumed, didn't know Him. Certainly, if the Mexicans were Catholic, they wouldn't have an authentic relationship with Christ.

Of course, the Mexicans spoke only Spanish and work team members only spoke English. The plan to "witness for Christ" was frustrated.

Communication was limited to sign language and some conversation through translators. The exciting result, though, was that relationships developed. Working together brought about a bonding and a mutual appreciation. David returned home full of excitement about what had happened. Love had abounded. Doctrine didn't get in the way, so relationships and love were built along with the houses throughout the week.

One should strive to love those immediately around them, including spouse, children, friends, neighbors, and associates. And, extending outward, love should include people throughout the city, state, and country. Jesus takes all the limits away. His teaching about love is all-inclusive. The love of Jesus includes and embraces everybody.

I remember a story told to me by a dear friend who was teaching a class of boys in Sunday school. The lesson was about loving enemies. The teacher asked the boys if they had an enemy. "Yes," they replied in unison, "Eddie!" She inquired about Eddie. It seems that he was a bully and the boys were completely intimidated by him.

"Well," the teacher told the boys, "the lesson today is clear that we are to love enemies and that includes Eddie. Let's have a prayer for him. Everyone bow your heads and we'll pray for Eddie."

She said all the boys dutifully bowed their heads and closed their eyes. Then, after a time of silence, each boy, one after the other, prayed the same simple prayer, "Lord, please change Eddie."

That is a simplistic, childish way to deal with those who are difficult or different . . . *Lord, change them.* Not me. Not us. Them. I am right and he is wrong. Lord, please help that misguided soul see the light. Change Eddie. Mary. Sally. Change all those people who are wrong.

In matters religious, there is the tendency to become rigid and dogmatic. Once that happens, love is usually a casualty. It is extremely difficult to love someone who, one is certain, is in profound sin or error. Love, especially directed toward those who are quite different from ourselves, is not easy. I believe it is only possible to practice such love by and through divine intervention. One must turn to God and pray for the strength to love and to love without limits.

Such a determination to love is so awesomely important, especially in the times in which we live, when the world is increasingly diverse and governments, groups, and individuals have access to awesome sources of destructive power. It seems that we must make a greater effort to love and respect one another. Not to make such an effort, it seems to me, will give even freer rein to hatred and all of the negative forces that such hatred unleashes.

Love is not easy. It requires determination and even suffering, as Christ demonstrated on the cross. But the alternative is so much worse.

We read in Romans that "Love does no harm to a neighbor; therefore love is the fulfillment of the law" (13:10). Love is so much better than anything else. Don't you agree? After all, as the thirteenth chapter of First Corinthians states so eloquently, "Now abide faith, hope, love, these three; but the greatest of these is love" (v. 13).

"The greatest." "Fulfillment of the law." It doesn't get any better or any higher than that.

Think of a person or a group of people for whom you have contempt or even hatred. Why do you feel as you do toward them? How can you change your feelings so that contempt and hatred are replaced by love?

The command is simple: LOVE! It is not always easy, but love anyway.

GENEROSITY

God loves a generous heart. I firmly and strongly believe that. Everything I have come to know and understand about God persuades me to believe that God loves and honors generosity. God, of course, is the ultimate giver. He is the source of life itself and all that we know in life. As a Christian, I understand and accept that God so loved the world that He gave His only begotten son . . . I would call that magnanimous act the ultimate in generosity. Since God is love and love is about giving, when a person is generous, he or she is close to the heart of God.

When Linda and I went through our marital crisis in the early years of our marriage, and we made the decision to divest ourselves of our wealth, we were drawn closer to each other, to our children, and to God. Also, we were drawn closer to many wonderful people outside our family. And the biggest bonus of all was that we were brought by God, we believe, into a work of building houses for families in need that evolved into the worldwide ministry that is known today as Habitat for Humanity.

What blessings and joys we have known in the years since our decision to give away our wealth! Of course, I do not say to every wealthy person that you should give away all that you have. I do say that *everyone* should listen to and respond to the still, small voice of God. He calls different people to different tasks and responsibilities. I say the wise person listens to God and responds to God's call. The details of one's response will vary from person to person and from situation to situation. However, I believe that God calls and expects from everyone, *generosity*. That generosity should permeate life and it should be lifelong.

Generosity has a lightness to it. When we are generous, something happens to us. We are blessed. Jesus said, "It is more blessed to give than to receive" (Acts 20:35). He did not say it is not blessed to receive, just *more* blessed to give. Often, sheer delight and long-lasting joy result from generosity.

I remember being on a plane during the time Linda and I were in the process of divesting ourselves of our wealth. A young woman sitting beside me poured out her heart about her boss. She said that his small company was about to go under for lack of capital. I asked her how much money he needed. She said that $25,000 would probably save the company. I told her to tell her boss that I would lend him the money. She was astounded. When we landed, I arranged to have the money sent to him, as an unsecured no-interest loan.

The money did save the man's company and, over time, he paid every penny of the money back, not to me but to charities I designated. I became friends with the man and we're still friends more than thirty years later. And he has been generous to others, too, as I was to him.

More recently, I was in New York at LaGuardia airport. I got off the plane and boarded a bus that transports passengers into Manhattan. I took a seat about halfway back in the bus. Other passengers boarded, including a middle-aged woman who took a seat near the front of the bus. The driver entered the bus and slowly made his way toward the back, collecting the bus fare from each passenger along the way. When he got to the middle-aged woman, an argument ensued. He wouldn't take her money. As the argument became more heated, other passengers joined in, "Get off the bus, lady, if you don't have the fare. You're holding up the bus."

Finally, the driver moved on past the woman. He didn't take her money and she didn't budge. He walked on back, collecting other fares along the way. When he got to me, I gave him the ten-dollar fare for myself and I asked what the problem was with the woman. He said she had Canadian money and he couldn't take it. I gave him another ten-dollar bill and said I would pay the fare for her. As he walked back past the woman, he nodded toward me and told the woman I had paid her fare. He took the driver's seat, and we headed off toward the city.

After we had traveled for a few minutes, the woman walked back and sat down in an empty seat across the aisle from me. "Why did you do that?" she asked.

"Two reasons," I responded. "First, I am a Christian and my religion teaches that I should help people, even strangers. Next, I wanted to get into the city and you were holding up the bus."

She burst into tears. She had on quite a bit of mascara and it started to streak down her face with the tears.

"I'm Jewish," she said.

"God loves Jews," I responded.

More tears came and more streaked mascara. She told me that she had just flown in from Canada and hadn't had time to change any money. A member of her family was gravely ill in the city, and she was distraught about that situation.

We continued to converse all the way into Manhattan. As we approached our destination, she asked for my name and address so she could send me the money I had paid for her fare. I refused to give her that information. She then wanted to know the name and address of my church so she could send a donation. I refused to give her that information as well.

"Why?" she wanted to know.

"Because," I replied, "the only way to pay me back is to help someone else someday who may need you."

The tears flowed again and down her face came the remaining mascara. That whole experience greatly blessed me and, I believe, it blessed her, too.

One of the most wonderful experiences I've had with generosity is when I was the recipient. When our family returned to the States in 1976 after serving three years as missionaries in Africa, I opened a small law office in Americus, Georgia, to provide a living for my family. At the same time, I convened a meeting at Koinonia Farm to organize and launch Habitat for Humanity.

Linda and I didn't have any money, but we did have four children to care for and educate. We had been sponsored as missionaries in Africa by the Christian Church (Disciples of Christ). The Division of Overseas Ministries (DOM) of that denomination was the specific entity that sent us out. They had a policy of continuing salary support for six months after returning from a three-year assignment. As that six-month period neared an end, I realized that I was still far from having enough income to support our family. My law practice was producing very little and Habitat for Humanity was minuscule in size. I asked the DOM to extend support for an additional six months. They knew our situation and that I was struggling not only to launch a law practice, but to start the new venture of Habitat for Humanity. The generous people of the church granted my request.

As that six-month period came to a close, I realized that I still was not making a living. I knew that I couldn't go back to the DOM. Instead, I contacted a dear friend, Bill Clarke, the owner of an electrical contracting company in Canton, Ohio. Bill had been involved in and supportive of Koinonia and I knew he felt fondly toward the new venture of Habitat for Humanity. I approached Bill with a most unusual request. I asked him to support my family for a year to enable me to "get on my feet" in the law practice and to firmly establish Habitat for Humanity.

Bill agreed. For a full year, he bought groceries, paid our house payments, bought our clothes, and covered all other expenses of our family. By the end of that year, my law practice was established and Habitat for Humanity was solidly up and running.

More than twenty years later, I spoke at a community-wide prayer breakfast in Canton that was attended by hundreds of people. With Bill Clarke present, I acknowledged his generosity to our family and to the fledgling ministry of Habitat for Humanity. It was a moment of great joy for me to be able to express public appreciation for what my dear brother had done for my family and me and for Habitat. I believe that experience was an equal joy to him. But, to be truthful, the joy for both of us had been ongoing since the moment of his generosity more than twenty years earlier.

These stories about generosity illustrate the importance and the blessings of a generous heart. It should be said, however, that generosity should not just be for unusual situations and individuals. Generosity should be a habit and it should be directed to our houses of worship, organizations, and causes in which we believe. Groups like Habitat for Humanity are almost solely dependent upon the generosity of people who regularly donate to the work. Churches and other such groups, both religious and secular, are, likewise, dependent on caring and generous people.

My advice is to develop a lifestyle of generosity, to individuals and organizations alike. If you do, you'll be blessed and so will the individuals and organizations who are the recipients of your generosity.

Are you a generous person? To whom and to what do you give? Is your giving restricted only to close friends and family? Should you reassess your giving pattern?

Do you generously and faithfully contribute to your church and to other organizations and causes in which you believe? Make a list of groups that you support with financial contributions. Should the list be expanded or reduced? Are the amounts you are giving about right or should they be adjusted up or down?

Also, are you generous in ways other than monetary? Do you share your time and make yourself available to others for conversation and companionship in a generous way?

Give of yourself and of your resources and you will be even more blessed than those who are the recipients of your generosity.

DELIGHT

Granddaughters Sophie and Jasmine were visiting with us at our home in Americus. One day I took Sophie fishing in a pond near our house. The very first time we put the hook in the water, she caught a small bream. It was probably no more than four inches long. But when that fish came out of the water and landed at her feet, flouncing around, she squealed to the top of her voice with total delight. It was a magical moment.

More recently, Linda and I were on the coast of Georgia, where I was writing this book. One afternoon, we went for a walk. Others were out walking, too, and still others were enjoying an outing by engaging in various activities. One man, probably a grandfather, was on the beach with a little girl. He was throwing a stick into the ocean. A beautiful Labrador retriever was faithfully fetching the stick and returning it. Just as we walked abreast of the man and girl, the dog ran up to them and dropped the stick at the girl's feet. She clenched up her fists, stomped the ground with her feet as fast as she could and squealed to the top of her lungs. Another expression of total delight. It was a blessing to witness that little drama.

The Bible talks about delight. The very first chapter of Psalms exclaims, "Blessed is the man who walks not in the counsel of the ungodly, nor stands in the path of sinners, nor sits in the seat of the scornful; but his delight is in the law of the Lord" (vv. 1-2). The fortieth chapter of Psalms restates basically the same thing, "I delight to do your will, O my God, and your law is within my heart" (v. 8). In the New Testament, Paul writes in Romans, "I delight in the law of God according to the inward man" (7:22).

A little girl delights in catching a fish or having a dog return a stick from the ocean. As adults, we, too, should continue to be delighted by the simple joys of life. But our greatest delight should be in doing God's will, in being faithful to God's law and Christ's teachings.

Jesus says that we cannot enter the kingdom of God unless we become as a little child. That means that the delight we experience in an innocent child should be embraced and expressed in our love of God and His way for us.

The person, I think, who best exemplifies delight in his life and ministry is Tony Campolo. Tony is a Baptist pastor and sociologist who teaches at Eastern College in St. David's, Pennsylvania. He travels and speaks constantly all over the world. I have had the privilege of being with Tony on numerous occasions. He seems to be perpetually delighted. His eyes dart from side to side as he tells you his latest funny story. And when he speaks, his whole demeanor is absolutely full of delight. He always delivers a serious message about Christ and His saving grace, but he fills his sermons with humor and childlike joy and delight. Anyone who knows Tony Campolo knows that he is a joyous person and he delights in doing God's work and in being God's messenger.

Is your life characterized by delight? Are you filled with a childlike delight by simple experiences of life? Or have you become a grump? Do you delight in doing God's will? Or have you become cynical and don't even care to know what God's will is for your life?

God certainly wants to delight in you. But God's delight is conditional on your seeking to know and do His will. Are you faithfully doing that? Is God delighted with you? If not, why not?

I believe you'll find that causing God to be delighted in you will fill you with delight as well. That seems like a good deal, don't you think?

CHERISH CHILDREN

When I was a little boy growing up in Lanett, Alabama, my dad, Render Fuller, owned and operated a small grocery store at the edge of town. One day, the pastor of our church was visiting with my father. The two of them were standing in front of the store as they carried on a conversation. I was there, full of energy, so I started picking up gravel from the yard and throwing the small stones across the highway. One of them almost hit a passing car. My father yelled at me, "Stop throwing those rocks! You almost hit that car."

My father then exclaimed to the pastor, "What am I going to do with this boy?" I'll never forget the reply of the pastor, "Render, don't worry about that boy. He and others like him are all we have to make men of."

Indeed, little boys and little girls are all we have to make men and women for the next generation. They should be cherished and nurtured, so they can be the best individuals possible.

Sometimes, the cherishing is easy. Recently, our youngest daughter, Georgia, was visiting with Linda and me at our home in Americus. With her were her two beautiful little daughters, Sophie and Jasmine. At the time, Sophie was three years old. One afternoon, I went on a walk with her. As we ambled along, she looked up at me and said, "Granddaddy, you're nice. I love you." My heart, already inclined so much toward love for her, totally melted. At times like that, nurturing and loving children is so easy.

On other occasions, children are not so sweet and nice. They yell and scream, make messes, get sick, cause trouble, and so much more. Even so, they should be loved, cherished, and appreciated in spite of everything and at all times.

So much can be learned from children. They have such refreshing insights and uncluttered views of the world. The way they express themselves can often be so creative and so different from conventional ways of expression.

One day, the child of a volunteer couple at Habitat in Americus passed gas quite loudly. He smiled broadly and exclaimed, "My body burped!"

Another time our son, Chris, who was about two years old at the time, fell out of his high chair. Fortunately, he was not hurt. He rose from the floor with a smile on his face. As he rubbed his little tummy and sides, making sure that he was okay, he announced, "Oops. I dropped myself!"

Young minds are unencumbered by all of the stuff that gets programmed into the minds and hearts of people as they grow up. I think it is that openness and unencumbered mind and heart that make them so open to God and to things of the spirit. I think that's why Jesus said that one must become like a little child to enter into the kingdom of Heaven.

A few years ago, I was in Daytona Beach, Florida, to participate in breaking ground for a new Habitat house to be built by the local affiliate. As a crowd gathered at the site, I was introduced to the family who had been chosen to live in the house. One member of the family was a cute little ten-year-old boy who was introduced to me as "Hamburger."

"Hamburger?" I inquired. "Is that your name?"

"Yes," he proudly replied. "I'm Hamburger."

"So, you want me to call you Hamburger?"

"Yes," he replied. "That's my name. I'm Hamburger."

I chatted with him and other family members until the program started, when I quickly learned that Hamburger was not shy. I wonder if any person named "Hamburger" could be shy or reserved in any way?

When my part on the program came, I said appropriate things for such an occasion. Then, seeing my new little friend "Hamburger" standing there, beaming from ear to ear, I spontaneously called him up to me. I faced him toward the lot where the house was to be built. At the time, the lot was full of weeds and an assortment of debris. Nothing had yet been done to get construction started.

"Hamburger," I asked, "As you look at this lot, what do you see?" I didn't know what he would say, but I felt that he would come up with something good and unusual.

He exceeded my expectations as he started describing a house that was not yet there. He could "see" it in his little mind. He described the house and talked about "his room." It was a special moment for me and others who were present.

As I left later that day, I reflected on what little Hamburger had said. I realized that he had vision. He could look at one thing and "see" something else.

About a year later, I got a letter from the director of Habitat in Daytona Beach. She told about the building of the house. And she enclosed a picture. It showed the lot where ground had been broken months earlier. The weeds were gone. The trash had been removed. In their place stood a beautiful house. Hamburger was standing in front of it, with a big smile on his face. The dream—his vision—had become real.

It gives me great joy to know that my little buddy, "Hamburger," will be able to grow up in that good, solid house *with his own room.*

I well remember another time in a very different and distant part of the world. Linda and I were in Uganda in east Africa, visiting Habitat's work in several locations in that country. We came to a small village and were introduced to a "widow and her orphans." They had recently moved into a new Habitat house and we were there to plant a tree in the front yard, present a Bible to the family, and dedicate the house.

I asked why the children were called orphans even though they were with their mother. We were told that in that part of the world, if there is not a father in the house, the children are called orphans because life is so difficult for the widow alone to provide for and raise the children.

The house was the ultimate in simplicity—about 500 square feet with an outdoor toilet, no electricity, and no plumbing. But it had a solid concrete floor, good strong block walls and a roof that would not leak. The woman was obviously thrilled to have the house.

As I spoke that day, I remembered the verse from the Bible that says, "Pure and undefiled religion before God is this: to visit orphans and widows in their trouble and to keep oneself unspotted from the world" (James 1:27). I began to weep, realizing that I was so privileged to be a part of "pure and undefiled religion."

One of my greatest joys is to realize that I have been a small part of helping to make life better for children by providing good houses for them and their parents in more than eighty nations. And more houses are being built for boys and girls and their families every few minutes.

Cherishing and nurturing children involves many things, but a good place to live is a big part of the whole process.

A SOFT ANSWER

A soft answer turns away wrath, but a harsh word stirs up anger. (Proverbs 15:1)

When Habitat for Humanity International first moved our headquarters into the city of Americus, Georgia, where we now operate, there was a row of derelict houses on a nearby street, occupied by low-income white families. Over the next few years, we systematically bought those houses, made necessary renovations, and moved Habitat volunteers into them. Finally, there was only one house left that was occupied by one of the original families.

Eventually, we moved an African American family into the house next door. The father of the white family was upset by having this black family next door to them. One afternoon, he drank several beers to bolster his courage. After he was sufficiently emboldened by the alcohol, he stormed into the front yard, yelling and screaming about how unhappy he was about the new neighbors.

Across the street lived Solomon Maendel, a big Hutterite man from South Dakota. Solomon and his family were with Habitat, working as volunteers. Solomon was as peaceful as any man could be, but he was big and strong, weighing more than 200 pounds. Solomon heard all of the commotion. He listened long enough to realize what the man was angry about. Solomon simply walked slowly and calmly across the street. Approaching the man, Solomon addressed him in a soft calm voice, "Joe," he said as he eased up to his side and placed his beefy arm around the man's neck, "you may not have noticed, but you are now surrounded by people who do not agree with you."

The man looked startled. Even though his mind was in somewhat of a fog because of all those beers, he still was able to realize that his neighbor had revealed something to him that he had not realized. Immediately, he began to calm down.

Solomon removed his arm from around the man's neck but kept talking to him in a calm voice. Within minutes, the crisis was completely over. And, interestingly enough, in the coming weeks, the man and his family became friends with the black family, even including visits in each other's houses.

On another occasion, I was in a Habitat International board meeting. A heated discussion was under way on some subject that I don't recall. A younger member of the board became a bit overheated about the matter and he raised his voice, gradually getting louder and louder. One of our older board members, a very distinguished and gracious southern lady, looked at the young man and firmly but softly spoke his name. That did it. The emotion dissipated.

The Bible promises that a soft answer turns away wrath. My experience is that it does indeed.

One of the most amazing "soft answer" solutions I've ever experienced happened in the early days of my law practice in Americus. A man came to my office one day with a complaint against one of his customers. The man was the owner of a roofing contracting company. He had put a new roof on a restaurant in town and, he said, the owner was refusing to pay for the work. The man told me that he had billed the restaurant owner several times and that she had not paid him a penny. As he talked to me about the matter, it was obvious to me that he was upset and angry, feeling that the woman was trying to cheat him.

I asked the man if I could simply phone the woman and make a demand for payment. I knew from experience that, often, if a person knows that a lawyer is in the picture, payment will be forthcoming. The man agreed for me to call her. I picked up the phone and dialed the number of the restaurant. The proprietor answered the phone. I told her who I was and asked for the payment. She told me that she wasn't paying because the roof leaked. She said that water poured right down on her grill in the kitchen when it rained and that there were other problems with the roof. I asked her if my client could come out and fix the problems. She quickly and firmly replied that she never wanted him on her roof again. She said he did an awful job, and she was disgusted with him and with his work.

When I reported to my client what she had said, he flushed with great anger. Then he thrust his head forward and with viciousness yelled, "I'll take care of this matter myself. I'm going home and get my pistol. Then, I'm going over to the restaurant and shoot that woman!"

In response to that outburst, I quietly asked, "Are you, by chance, a Christian?" A look of shock registered on his face. He slumped down in the chair and started breathing heavy. After several long seconds, he looked back up at me and said, "I gave my life to Jesus just a few weeks ago. I was baptized and became a Christian."

"What?" I replied. "You are a Christian and you are going to go kill someone?"

"No," he quietly responded. "I've committed a great sin. I have already killed that woman in my heart. I must ask God to forgive me. Please call the woman back and tell her that I give her the roof."

With that, he walked out of my office. Later, through the woman's lawyer, I was able to work out an equitable payment for my client's work. I did that on my own. He absolutely was willing to forego any payment. In any event, I do believe a possible murder was averted by my simple and "soft response" question to the angry man.

Everyone, at one time or another, has to deal with emotional and volatile situations. A soft answer is usually the best approach to calming things down, just as the book of Proverbs teaches.

Are you currently dealing with an emotional situation in your life? As you face it, remember the wise counsel of the Bible about the "soft answer" and the great danger of harsh words.

FORGIVENESS

You, Lord, are good, and ready to forgive. (Psalm 86:5)

If you forgive men their trespasses, your heavenly Father will also forgive you. But if you do not forgive men their trespasses, neither will your Father forgive your trespasses. (Matthew 6:14-15)

The Bible is full of teachings about forgiveness, but I think these two Scriptures encapsulate the essence of those teachings. God is good and ready to forgive. That is such good news because we humans are so subject to going astray. We are full of good and love and kindness but also endowed with a darker side. As the Bible says, "all we like sheep have gone astray" (Isaiah 53:6). We all stand in need of forgiveness, and the wonderful news is that God is good and ready to forgive.

But there are two preconditions to *actually* receiving forgiveness from God. First, you must sincerely desire to be forgiven. If you are in denial about your conduct and say, "I've done nothing wrong," then forgiveness will not be forthcoming from God. Our heavenly Father does not force-feed forgiveness to anyone. Second, you must forgive those who have wronged you. It is impossible to get forgiveness from God if you are unwilling to forgive people who have wronged you.

Now, how does this forgiveness work? In Luke, Jesus says, "If your brother sins against you, rebuke him; and if he repents, forgive him. And if he sins against you seven times in a day, and seven times in a day returns to you, saying, 'I repent,' you shall forgive him" (17:3-4). As you can clearly see, the principle set forth in Psalms and Matthew is stated in Luke. A person should *always* be *ready to forgive*. But, just as God cannot force someone to desire forgiveness, neither can another person. No person has control over another's heart and thoughts. You can have influence, but final control over all matters lies within the heart and mind of each individual.

So, where there has been a wrong or a hurt, the wronged person is counseled by Christ himself to have a completely sincere heart and mind of forgiveness and that mindset should be open-ended. One gets the impression from the passage in Luke that the willingness to forgive should be endless. If the offender turns to you and expresses regret and desire to be forgiven, then it should be forthcoming immediately.

It is impossible to go through life with numerous relationships—ranging from casual friendships to very deep ones, family relationships to business and social relationships, as well as the deepest relationship of all, marriage—without causing offense. The only question is how you put things right again after there have been offenses.

Linda and I have been married for more than forty years. On several occasions in our marriage, I have offended Linda and on other occasions she has offended me. Even so, after more than four decades of being married, we are not only still together—we love and adore one another. The secret has always been sharing everything with nothing withheld, and a *readiness to forgive*. That attitude has enabled wrongs to be put behind us so that they do not become blockades between us.

Forgiveness is not easy, especially when there has been a grievous wrong committed. Often, a person will ask for forgiveness and either that person is not sincere or the other person *perceives* that there is a lack of sincerity. Or, the offended party will accept an apology and request for forgiveness only to hold back in some way "just to make sure" the person really meant what he or she said. This "holding back" often poisons the atmosphere of the relationship.

Forgiveness, to work, must be sincere and without reservations. As I said above, that's not easy! Unfortunately, some broken relationships in life never get mended. In the Bible, it is reported that a rift developed between Paul and Barnabus. There is no record of them ever getting back together again.

I have some broken relationships in my life. I regret every one of them, but, for one reason or another, they just don't seem to get restored. Occasionally, a long broken relationship comes back. That's always cause for rejoicing.

I had such an experience very recently. This person was cut off from me completely for more than ten years. Then, out of the blue came a letter stating a desire to restore the relationship. I was so pleased by the dramatic turn of events. I have not yet seen this previously estranged person, but we have now exchanged several letters, and I know it's only a matter of time until the relationship is completely restored to the previous state of harmony and complete friendship.

Ready to forgive is God's orientation, as stated at the outset of this chapter. It ought to be yours, too. *Ready to forgive* is the best way to live.

Do you have any broken relationships in your life? Would you like to see those relationships restored? What could you do to begin the process of restoration? Have you wronged someone? Have you been wronged? Are you ready and willing to seek forgiveness and to forgive?

It is incredibly difficult to ask for forgiveness, and it is equally hard to actually forgive, but taking those difficult steps can be both painful and rewarding. Are you willing to take a risk and venture into those uncertain waters? If you forgive and seek forgiveness to heal a broken relationship, you may be surprised by incredible joy. And, in the same way, God forgives you.

PEACE WITHIN

Peace I leave with you, My peace I give to you; not as the world gives do I give to you. Let not your heart be troubled, neither let it be afraid. (John 14:27)

Have you ever felt your stomach churning, or your heart pounding from uneasiness or anxiety? Have you ever found your mind racing in a futile attempt to deal with a problem or situation that seems to defy solution? I think just about everyone can affirm that such a condition has prevailed at one time or another.

A troubled heart and a frightened mind are common to our human condition. We know that such a condition is not at all conducive to happiness or even to a state of mind that permits normal activities to be carried out. Peace is a highly desired state of being, both external and internal. The profound question is how to achieve it.

In this Scripture, Jesus says clearly that He is the source of peace. "Peace I leave with you," he proclaims, "My peace I give to you." It is a free gift. There is no need to struggle for it. There is no requirement that you pass a "peace test" or pay some price or perform some act to be entitled to peace. It is simply and abundantly given. So open your heart and your mind and receive the great gift of peace from Jesus.

"But," you exclaim, "How?" The Bible says, "Be still and know that I am God" (Psalm 46:10).

One of the most powerful stories in Scripture comes from the book of 1 Kings. God commands Elijah to go stand on a mountain. First, a great and strong wind tears into the mountains and breaks the rocks in pieces. But, the story boldly asserts, the Lord is not in the wind. Then an earthquake hits, but the Lord is not in the earthquake. Next comes a fire, but the Lord is not in the fire. Finally, after the fire, there is a still small voice (19:11-12).

The contrast is so powerful. Wind, earthquake, fire! All noisy, destructive forces. The opposite of peace. Then all of a sudden, a still small voice.

Listen. Be still. Be attentive. In the wake of all the calamities and chaos and confusion and disruptive things in life, there is that still small voice. It is the voice of God. It is Jesus standing at your heart's door, offering you peace. Receive it. What a great gift!

Of course, receiving the peace of Christ into your life does not mean that no more calamities will come along. Life is a jumble. Death and disease, disappointments and setbacks are common in human experience, and such things do not subside after one has received the gift of peace from Jesus. But a peaceful, calm heart enables one to better deal with the vicissitudes of life.

The external world is not peaceful. There are wars and rumors of wars. Thieves and robbers and violence of all sorts are around us. We struggle, or we should struggle, to help make the world a more peaceful place, but our internal state is more under our control. When we accept the gift of peace from Christ, we are better equipped to deal with an external lack of peace.

I remember standing on a curb near the capitol building in Montgomery, Alabama, in March of 1965 when Martin Luther King, Jr. passed by, leading the civil rights marchers on the final leg of their long march from Selma to Montgomery. I'll never forget the serene look on his face. He was at the center of swirling activity, much of it hate-filled. A man near me had a pistol, and he wanted to shoot the marchers. His face was anything but peaceful.

I got the strong impression that Dr. King had spent time in quiet reflection about what he was doing. He knew the dangers. He was aware of the forces arrayed against him and his movement, but he believed in the rightness of his cause. I believe he had invited Jesus to give His peace to him. He was a man of peace, at peace, even as he struggled against great forces to change an external situation to make things better for his people.

That awesome peace that was given to Dr. Martin Luther King, Jr. is available to all. God's desire is for all to know Him and to have His peace, the peace that passes all understanding.

Let not your heart be troubled, neither let it be afraid. Receive the gift of peace that is so freely and abundantly given. Receive and pass it on. Blessed are the peacemakers. Blessed are you when you are filled with the peace of Christ, which enables you to engage a troubled and violent world and maintain your serenity in the midst of whatever swirls around you.